S0-AYX-828

SPRING 60

A JOURNAL OF

ARCHETYPE

AND

CULTURE

Fall, 1996

SPRING PUBLICATIONS

WOODSTOCK, CONNECTICUT 06281

ACKNOWLEDGMENTS

To Princeton University Press for quotations from the *Collected Works (CW)* of C. G. Jung (Bollingen Series XX), translated by R. F. C. Hull, edited by H. Read, M. Fordham, G. Adler, and Wm. McGuire, and published in Great Britain by Routledge and Kegan Paul, London. Other quotations have been acknowledged throughout in appropriate notes and references.

Spring is the oldest Jungian journal in the world. It was founded in 1941 by the Analytical Psychology Club of New York. In 1970, James Hillman transferred its editing and publication to Zürich, Switzerland. From 1978 to 1988, it was edited in Dallas, Texas. Since 1988 it has been edited in Connecticut.

CONTENTS

MARRIAGES: Editors' Note

JAMES HILLMAN
Marriage, Intimacy, Freedom   1

NOR HALL
Architecture Of Intimacy   13

JOSEPH J. LANDRY
"Marriage Is Impossible!"
Scattered Thoughts Of A Married Man   27

NANCY TENFELDE CLASBY
Realism And The Archetypes: *Daisy Miller*   31

GINETTE PARIS
If You Invite The Gods To Your Marriage   47

RACHEL POLLACK
Breaking The Will Of Heaven:
The Abduction/Marriage Of Hades And Persephone   55

C. L. SEBRELL
Marry The Gardener!   75

HELEN G. HENLEY
from What Can We Ask Of Marriage?   83

EREL SHALIT
An Interview From Israel   93

JAMES HILLMAN
"Psychology—Monotheistic Or Polytheistic":
Twenty-Five Years Later   111

SHEILA GRIMALDI-CRAIG: (BOOK REVIEWS)
Youthful Illusion   127

SPRING 60: MARRIAGES

Woody Allen once said, "Marriage is the death of hope." Like most Woody Allenisms, the statement is only briefly amusing. And if you don't immediately shrug it off as a joke, the thought can become downright depressing. Thus, depending on your point of view, the following statistic from the United States Department of Health and Human Resources is either very alarming, or very encouraging: The marriage rate in the United States rose to 9.1 marriages per thousand people in 1994. This represents an increase of 10 percent since 1990. Hopelessness, or a sign of greater responsibility?

Because the subject has become particularly embattled of late, with politicians of all stripes feeling they have to champion "family values" against some nameless enemy, we are devoting this issue of *Spring* to a discussion of marriages, or at least to certain aspects of them that fall into the inhuman purview of archetypal psychology, such questions as what happens to intimacy as a result of marriage, and is it the fault of the architecture? why do some people feel they have lost their freedom after they are married, and is there a God in this fantasy that might be of help? if you do invite the Gods to your marriage, what happens next? ("Trouble," says Ginette Paris.)

Marriage has of course come a long way in the nearly fifty years since we first published an article by Helen Henley, called "What Can We Ask of Marriage?" That article opens with a sentence that Mrs. Henley, and the other members of the Analytical Psychology Club of New York to whom she read the paper, took to be an unshakable certainty. "Marriage is the foundation stone upon which rests almost every culture of every tribe or nation that treads this earth." For Mrs. Henley, "the bonds of matrimony are too easily rent asunder." Her thoughts are guided throughout by Jung's words, that "Individuation always means relationship." But relationship, of course, doesn't always mean individuation, and there the trouble seemed to lie, at least in 1949. Today, with the American divorce rate soaring, we re-print some of Mrs. Henley's thoughts for the record, the archeological record of "Fifty Years Ago in *Spring*" if nothing else.

Mrs. Henley's paper does not, at least, take marriage *literally*. Literally, the word "marriage" derived from the French word for "husband," and "matrimony" itself derived from a Latin word for "motherhood." In its most fundamental and literal sense, marriage was strictly for the production of legitimate babies. (Those seeking to legalize Gay marriages today in the United States are up against such literalists, or at least the element of marriage literalists who are content that their position is also a lucrative way of denying health benefits to Gay spouses while continuing to collect full payment from Gay workers themselves.)

Regular readers of *Spring* surely realize that if there is some subject out there that we can help to deliteralize, it will be set upon like hounds to gooseliver. (Well, maybe not quite so inelegantly.) Marriage is no exception, and we think you will find this issue full of challenges no matter what your position is.

So, while marriage may well be "the death of hope," you must know by now that hope was never one of our favorite virtues in the first place.

— *The Editors*

MARRIAGE, INTIMACY, FREEDOM

JAMES HILLMAN

The force of the title—those three little words, "Marriage, Intimacy, Freedom," so like those other three words, "I Love You," strike such deep chords. What an extraordinarily powerful fantasy is here at work! How much longing is stirred! O, if only...

I say fantasy with deliberate purpose, for we each know from the facts of our lives that Marriage is often dull, banal, and also a crux of agony; Intimacy brings us to stammers, complaints and tears; and Freedom, as Erich Fromm said fifty years ago, is one of humankind's greatest fears.

So the actualities of marriage, of intimacy, of freedom as events we try to live in practice and clarify in concepts are quite distinct from the hopes and longings generated in the soul by the fantasies of Marriage, Intimacy and Freedom. Just here is the mystery: the strange disjunction between Fact and Fantasy, and just here is the misery, trying to force the facts to fit the fantasy, or sardonically abandoning the fantasy altogether.

We shall have to ask what does the soul want that it sets us so on expectation's edge? What is this response in the heart that brings us to long for a new marriage, a better marriage, a different

James Hillman is the Senior Editor of this journal. This paper is a revised version of a keynote talk to a conference with this title at the Dallas Institute of Humanities and Culture in October, 1993. The paper is now dedicated to the late Robert Stein, who also presented at the conference.

marriage, more true intimacy, and for freedom? Why these three terms? Why not three older Republican ones—Marriage, Children, Family? Or newer ones: Relationship, Divorce, Selfhood; or just two: Intimacy and Freedom; why throw in Marriage? Might there be a way to maintain the ideal fantasies toward which we long when we hear these words without succumbing to the difficult facts in which the words are embedded, especially the facts of marriage?

In responding to the three themes of the title, I beg incompetence. It is as if I strayed into a dream where I must discuss in a foreign language a topic about which I haven't a clue. Freedom? I am Mr. Bourgeois, guilt-loaded with obligations, reduced by anxieties about promises and schedules, chained by habits and taxes and stick-in-the-mud routines, hemmed in by the conventions of consumer values, cosmetic appearances, and hypochondriacal worries. Freedom!

As for Intimacy, I run from it. It's none of your business. I often pronounce in print against contemporary cults of intimacy, the sharing, confessing and revelatory glimpses of inconsequential childhood. I consider our civilization to be caught up in the minutiae of intimate biography, people wanting to gossip about themselves (not even about their neighbors) and then calling this gossip "recovery." All this intimacy in a world where there are dire and desperate public matters waiting.

Marriage—I've tried it. Indeed I've been married more years of my life than I've been single, and those were the main mature *conscious* years. But I haven't a clue what makes it work and not work, discern which is which, or whether that word "work" is applicable at all.

Perhaps I hesitate to discuss marriage because I look to the Greeks for archetypal patterns. Except, perhaps, for Philemon and Baucis, horror stories: Clytemnestra; Medea and Jason; Phaedra and the mess in that household; Priam and his concubines; the frustrated husbands of the *Lysistrata*. Think of Socrates and Xantippe. As for that pop version of a devoted couple (Penelope and Ulysses), he caved in with Calypso for seven years while she was entertaining in their house innumerable nameless "suitors." Besides, is that a marriage when the couple are apart for twenty years! The great Goddesses—Artemis, Athene, Aphrodite, Hestia—stayed clear of marriage, while the marriage of Persephone and Hades was spent one third of the time in Hell, among specters of the dead and no daylight.

Solon the lawmaker is said to have refused to set rules for marriage. He was so down on it that he regarded woman a deadweight on a man's life. Plato and Lycurgus took marriage only as duty; their laws insist men marry for the state's sake, and they order punishment for those who marry late or never. Plutarch warns of money-marriage and uses the image of chains for a marriage to a rich woman. Besides these cautions for men, feminism has well laid bare the misery of marriage for women in antiquity.

Zeus and Hera, however, offer a more complex and entertaining story. Cheap editions that tell us he was a philanderer, a real "animal," and she a furiously possessive virago, miss the fact that together as a syzygy they present the archetypal tension, so crazy to live, of all our three themes. They do have intimacy, but her idea of marriage is set against his idea of freedom; while her idea of freedom is to do her own thing all by herself apart from marriage. Our human limits do not let us hold what Zeus and Hera can combine. They go on eternally in their bind; we divorce. So, I want to find other patterns, other myths. For once to be free of the Greeks.

We are already into one of our topics: Freedom. Let's go on with it. How do we usually imagine it: a bird's wing, Hermes' light heels, flitting, puer, trickster-escapes, escape-artist, unhampered libidinal arousal. Unimpeded, uninhibited, unpredictable, untrammeled, unbound. Don't fence me in. Free-wheeling, freeloading, freebooter. Is this the vision of freedom informing the minds of the founders of our Republic?

In his recent book, *From the Wrong Side*,[1] Adolf Guggenbühl-Craig entitled a chapter "Creativity, Spontaneity, Independence: Three Children of the Devil." He lays out quite ruthlessly how dangerous and anti-social are these shibboleths of current human-

---

[1]Adolf Guggenbühl-Craig, *From The Wrong Side: A Paradoxical Approach to Psychology*, trans. Gary V. Hartman with a commentary by Sidney Handel (Spring Publications: Woodstock, Connecticut, 1995).

istic psychology. He shows how our devotion to independence denies the simple truth that we are each deeply and necessarily dependent on one another and, I add, the environments that sustain our lives. He also makes clear that the spontaneity of freedom may be cruelly destructive. Many acts of violence—rapes, beatings, suicides, homicides—occur suddenly, spontaneously. Free acts. What the French call *l'acte gratuite*, may arise as an impulse from the savage soul, undomesticated or demonic. To be free is not necessarily to be good.

Yet what does the soul—which speaks sometimes most accurately in the depths of language—want with that word Freedom which sets off such expectations? What sort of preposition accompanies and influences Freedom? Freedom *from*—from fear, want, and oppression, such as enunciated by the Charter that established the United Nations after World War Two? Or is it freedom *of*—choice, opportunity and movement, or access in today's political language?

Or, is it rather Freedom *to*: to do as I like, to hire whom I want, to tell the boss to shove it, to go where I want, to marry whom I please—a freedom of agency in the empowered and recovered adult of therapy?

Or, fourth, is it possibly Freedom *in*? This seems moronic or oxymoronic, for the fantasy of American, epitomized by Texan, freedom is "don't fence me in." "In" means within limits or constraints of any place, time, situation, condition, such as in the kitchen, in an hour, in a conversation, in a marriage.

This fourth preposition, "in," rather than freedom of, to and from, suggests that the joyful expectation arising in the soul when the bell of freedom rings is nothing other than living fully in the actuality of this or that situation, as it is, which gives to that situation wings, freeing it from the desire to be elsewhere, to escape from it, to want more, thereby sating the soul's desire with the fullness of the present. How do we say it? "I love what I'm doing...I'm fully in it." "I'm really into tex-mex cooking; my new computer; re-painting the house." Is this compulsion? Addiction? Or is it the freedom given with passionate love?

Here by the way is what the soul, via its invention of language, says about freedom: the Indo-European root of Free is *pri*, love, from which, Freya, the Nordic-Teutonic Goddess of Love, Fria, Friday Free-day, just as Liberty the latinate equivalent, comes from the Italic God Liber, who blended with the Greek Diony-sos, the free-flow of liquid saps contained in the plant world, the sexual stuff in the marrow of the animal, the liberal loosening within any moment, place, or condition, the moment we feel how we love it and it loves us. Yes, a liberal must be a big spender and free lover just as the right-wing declares. Etymology is also politics.

By locating the source of freedom in the love Goddesses Frigg and Freya and the figure of Liber, I am decoupling the idea of freedom from the human individual. I am dehumanizing it. That historical location of freedom with the personal "me," for all its liberating and dignifying advantages, has also resulted in Western competitive atomism, each of us straining for esteem and empow-erment by asserting his and her rights. Such free individuals like free radicals, combine into no communities until forced by a so-cial contract which protects that person's freedom in exchange for submission to the contract. Otherwise life would be brutish, nasty and short (Hobbes).

Logically, then, freedom *from*, *of* and *to* depend on the prior preposition *in*—buying into the contract, being in the *polis*. Only then are you free from fear and able to do what you can. Partici-pation in the collective affirms your actual self which I have de-fined elsewhere as the internalization of community. You are your city. So, collective participation, *pace* Jung, is not the price of freedom but its true ground. Freedom is assured less by exer-cising your individual will in distinction to all others and more by belonging to the other. Myths express this innate belonging as brother-sister marriage; for instance, Zeus and Hera. Our mar-riage ceremony calls it "cleaving," "'til death us do part."

Belonging inherently in the other could also be called intimacy as described by the dictionary: a deep and extensive familiarity with; close; thoroughly mixed and united. I am implying now that our marriages can be relieved of that defensive stance of a nuclear twosome, defending privacy against collective infringe-ment. Two homesteaders on the prairie, away, alone, apart, shotgun cradled, standing guard. That steadfast marriage implies a bad world.

Inherently separated individuals cannot "marry" without giving up their individualistic definition of freedom. So our marriages don't "work," and neither does societal freedom. The more "freedom" our nation advocates, the more we invent regulations of it: wire-tapping, security surveillance, anti-Freeman measures, more imprisonments per capita than any nation on earth, longer school hours and curfews on youth, more credentials and permits and licenses, as well as politically corrective pressures of every sort that curtail and inhibit. We are caught in an unfixable dilemma: the more we affirm personal freedom the less of it we have. The more we demand guarantees from society, the less we feel freedom to be our own. What begins as personally innate and inalienable has come to depend on impersonal and alien systems.

I think this distortion of freedom derives from those three prepositions we already mentioned—freedom from, of and to. For these prepositions tie freedom with choices—as if more choices, the more freedom; tie it with need gratification—as if the faster and fuller a gratification, the more freedom; tie it with opportunities to enact fantasies—as if the more we can do, the freer we are. Surely, an exhausting program of multiple choices, speeded satisfactions and hyper-activity. Rather like American consumerism, which fosters neither marriage nor intimacy.

The only way I can imagine fixing the unfixable is to connect freedom with that fourth preposition, in. Only by shifting the idea of freedom to a base in myths and figures of the soul, as a cosmic ferment innate, might freedom be realized in its original sense of an ecstatic, orgasmic potential that vitalizes any choice, satisfaction or opportunity. This libidinal notion of freedom was developed by the Freudian left of Reich, Marcuse and Norman Brown, and witnessed long before it entered their minds by Christian, Sufi and Hassidic mystics in their exalted and tortured delights.

Freedom as the inmost juice of intimate love, the Goddess Freya in any moment able to bless any situation, leads us straight to Intimacy as the place where freedom can fully flourish. Opening the heart, the belly, the mind, via the mouth. Don't stop flow. Released libido—libido from *lips* [Greek], downpouring, outpouring. "I have never said this before." "Tell me, say anything you want." "I feel freer than ever in my life." "Do whatever you want with me." "Let go, let go." These are the speeches of intimacy—and of freedom. No wonder Freud's "talking cure" worked in nineteenth-century bourgeois Vienna: it offered freedom and intimacy both. To say whatever comes into your mind without restraint invites Freya onto the couch. Of course what came out was erotic, sexual. Not the later Apollonian analysis of the speech or an Oedipal *heuriskein* (figuring our your past deeds to "know yourself"), but Liber loosed, the loosening of the mouth as wine and whiskey loosen the tongue. Aphrodite loosening the girdle; Dionysos, "the Loosener." (And Dionysos, you will remember, was both Lord of Souls and only the God, other than Zeus, who had one wife, Ariadne, with whom he stayed married.)

Therapy supposedly gives you leave to be just as you want to be, utterly free, and supposedly loved for you as you are. This word "leave," to have leave, to take leave, to go on leave or on liberty—all lead back to the same meaning of love. For the words "leave" and "believe" are cognates of love. Intimacy gives leave to state one's love and one's inmost belief. Do you see why it is easy to fall in love with therapy, with the therapist? And why when you fall out of love, you no longer believe in therapy?

That intimacy has a sexual meaning is archetypally and mythically appropriate. "Did you have intimate relations?" asks the trial attorney, the news reporter. Intimacy meaning sexual relations; genital relations; intercourse as communion of the liquid sap of life. "Free," from Freya and Frigg; those Norse Goddesses derive their names from the same Indo-European root, *prij*, love, and *prij* is also the root of prick and Priapos. "Friend," too, comes from this root, that friend with whom you can be truly intimate.

Freya travels in a carriage pulled by pussycats. Other names configurate her as a fertile sow, as liquid manure, and the riches of the fecund earth of horse stall and barnyard. Intimacy invites in the vital sweet and smelly fantasies that are the inward riches of freedom.

These Goddesses of freedom, Freya and Frigg, also provide the blessings of marriage in Norse mythology. Imagine: freedom and marriage under the same aegis! Within this configuration a stable marriage would be indeed a stable marriage. Marriage thus becomes the place of both freedom and intimacy, the place where permission is given for the prick, the sow, and the pussycat, where "you have my leave" to be as you are, a leave that is the essence of love. To grant leave is to give love. The blessed state of matrimony therewith blesses all the priapic barnyard liberties of intimate life.

Well—so it might seem from the etymology and the mythology, but we do not live any longer among the Vikings, or the peoples of Italy for whom Liber was a friendly force. Dionysos has become a drunk, an unstopped tongue at an A. A. meeting. Our language has been Christianized along with our lands and our customs. So, when couples try to shed that Christianization in order to follow their bliss by living out the pagan myths—as did D. H. Lawrence and Frieda (*nomen est omen*)—they may find themselves more likely racked on the Cross than frolicking with Frigg.

Marriage today owes more to St. Paul than to Freya, Paul who said it is better to marry than to burn. Marriage is where the fires of ecstatic freedom dampen into the pallor of ash, where intimacy is only a carnal necessity for procreation, and where the passion of extra-marital and pre-marital fantasies of intimacy and freedom are burned away. Marriage as burn-out. Marriage as the big chill. Which then leads to the idea of personal freedom as escape from marriage. Robert Stein in his classic book *Incest and Human Love*,[2] and in his several writings in issues of this journal, calls this urge—and problem—"de-coupling." De-coupling offers a fantasy of intimacy *outside* of marriage in such extra-marital places as the therapist's office rather than under the comforter of the marriage bed.

Stein, a lovely man and a boldly original and sensitive therapist, said for years that the basic problems we meet in therapy, the ba-

---

[2]Robert Stein, *Incest and Human Love: The Betrayal of the Soul in Psychotherapy*, 2nd ed. (Spring Publications: Dallas, 1973; rpt. 1984).

sic messes of human lives, begin in marriage. I agree with him because marriage which is an archetypal mess to begin with—as a conjunction of incompatible opposites—is made yet more insupportable by our repressive negativist Pauline version of this conjunction. The blessed—and wherever there are blessings there are cursings too—state of matrimony is theologically cursed from the start. Even its intimacy has been lessened; so often what one brings to it from the most sacred place of the soul is feared by the other as a threat. "I could never tell this to my wife." "My husband simply doesn't want to hear about such things..."

We hold back from each other and suspect each other instead; thereby a cold bed of marriage becomes a hotbed of jealousy. We forget that marriage, by its very oath of better and worse is a sanctuary where exposure is not only allowed but absolutely mandatory. Thus, Felix Pollak's poem, "The Dream[3]:"

> He dreamed of
> an open window.
> A vagina, said
> his psychiatrist.
> Your divorce, said
> his mistress.
> Suicide, said
> an ominous voice within him.
> It means you should close the window
> or you'll catch cold, said
> his mother.
> His wife said nothing.
> He dared not tell her
> such a
> dangerous dream.

We keep our marriages going by repression. No wonder freedom and intimacy become its opposites.

Finally, now, I believe that beyond Marriage, Intimacy, Freedom, there lurks a fourth and hidden term. For a Jungian there is always a hidden fourth. Within and behind the aspiring expectations of the soul is a haunting sadness from which our three

---

[3]Felix Pollak, *Subject to Change* (Juniper Press, 1978).

themes offer seductive solutions. I am referring to the human condition of loneliness.

We have been living in a century of increasing loneliness borne out by demographic statistics that show the breakup of large families living together, the divorce rate, the women who must work to maintain the nation's unjust trickle-down economics, alienation of adolescents, prolongation of existence for the aged, separatist racist practices, tremendous mobility of the population, and all the other sociological statistics testifying to loneliness. The current idealization of "community" and the therapeutic shibboleths about "relationship" bear further witness to an underlying isolation of individuals.

Isn't this loneliness cosmological? Doesn't it come with our *Weltbild*? Like atoms rapping in a void: we may be attracted to and repelled by one another, but we are inherently unrelated. Isn't our loneliness epistemological? For we are but a pair of perceiving eyes, protruding from a processing brain observing a world we inhabit though not necessary to it. Loneliness comes with how we have mapped the territory, so loneliness can hardly be remedied by personal measures. No marriage, no intimacy and no exercise of personal freedom can reach its roots which extend throughout Western cosmology.

And so, your loneliness and mine tell of a more fundamental separation—that exile from the cosmos itself, from the Gods and daimones and ancestors, and from the rituals that keep the world, that is also their world, intimately shared. Inside your and my desire for relationship is that longing for relationship with them, while our call for community yearns for communion with them who sustain life, give our lives their myths, provide its truths, inhabit its nature and govern its works.

They do not guarantee blessing—again witness the Greeks. Destruction and disaster also issue from their hands. And, they are certainly not free in any drive-by or any Texan sense of freedom, for the Gods too are bound by cosmic order. At least, however, intimacy with them ameliorates the yearning that we bring to the fantasy of marriage and which its facts do not assuage. Just this loneliness, this search for sheltering union, as Robert Stein revealed so poignantly in his writings, makes our all-too-human marriages fall apart and enlarges the delusion that to be "unmarried" is to find intimacy and be free, both.

Though I cannot fix what is wrong or state what is right, I may at least plead for that little preposition *in*. The more we stay in and the further we go in, the more freedom we may find and the more Gods we may discover. The *in* side of marriage would be like that startling depiction of Socrates at the end of the *Symposium* [217a] (a dialogue about love and intimacy). The "ugly" casing of the human (Socrates) has "little images inside...so godlike, so golden, so beautiful and so utterly amazing."

This is the intimacy we covet and may find—intimacy with them "so utterly amazing," and also with them in their monstrous shapes, relieving the personal of demands to cure marriage of its peculiarities and pathologies. You can't cure the Gods—so lay off trying to change your partner. Intimacy with them invites a freedom of commerce between their world and ours, between human and inhuman, between fantasy and fact. The impersonal inhuman immortals take up rooms in the personal frailties of the human household, sharing bed and board, and boredom, freeing the householders of working so hard at the marriage. I think this is what the married soul most wants.

ARCHITECTURE OF INTIMACY

NOR HALL

"Thus we cover the universe with drawings we have lived."
--Gaston Bachelard

A "dream house" is, sadly, often not a house capable of dreaming. Dream houses should be dwellings with centers of solitude, centers of boredom, and centers of daydreaming that nourish the imagination, rather than houses of wishful thinking that spring from a romantic delusion. The Ladies Magazine picture that rose up white-washed and perfect in collective imagination earlier in this century registered the desire for an ideal home during the War and the Great Depression. Couples who had insurmountable distances placed between them by poverty, or by being shipped overseas, were linked in the imagination by the fantasy of an abundant and peaceful life together. Our fantasy could be perfect if only the image were just so—the perfect mate, the perfect wedding, the perfect house.

This blueprint for happiness that has been handed down to us, comes from our childhoods, and from the childhood of the twentieth century—and does not work.

"...dwelling is not primarily inhabiting, but taking care of and creating a space in which something comes into its own and flourishes."   —Heidegger

Nor Hall "dreams up unusual structures for archetypal relationships in St. Paul, Minnesota and all over the world." These designs were first shown at the Dallas Institute conference on Marriage.

An unusual teacher once piled his fifth grade class into a van (including me) and drove us to the outskirts of an old New Jersey town where he stopped in the middle of a new housing development and asked us to look around. The houses sat in a row, neat as a pin, exactly the same size: uniform issue houses for a couple, two children, and their attached cars. Then he drove back into the central neighborhoods to show us the older, colonial houses on irregular, deep lots. Houses with porches, odd protrusions, outside staircases, generally housed more than four people. They could include extended families of all sizes and shapes. The yards were variously tended, but each held some set-apart space: a clump of trees, a potting shed, a fishpool, a daffodil circle—places for the imagination to dwell. The newer houses in the "development" looked stark and lonely in contrast: isolated, inorganic, finalized, and therefore, dead.

Those houses in the suburbs were turned in on themselves in a physically confining design, generating an unnatural involution in relationships. A natural dwelling, on the other hand, would facilitate a coming together in an organic, reverse spiral form that creates movement in the space surrounding the partners. Leading us to ask, "Is marriage natural?"

begonia leaf

Or is it "unnatural," as Vita Sackville-West and Harold Nicholson said in their 1929 BBC interview: "Marriage is only tolerable for people of strong character and independent minds if it is regarded as a lifetime association between intimate friends. Each must be supple and subtle...And the bond should last only as long as both want it to." Relationships that work allow room for the imaginal requirements of all parties involved. Otherwise the unmet imagination will begin devising a fantasy of a way out—and the life it seeks will always be elsewhere. Souls trapped in soulless arrangements tend to lose their capacity for envisioning how this particular space could be any different. When changes in our dwelling shells do occur they are not random. A simple example: the couple who build a skylight into the ceiling of their bedroom try to turn the tide of relationship by making a spirit-window (like the ones still visible in European church towers) where there was only space for heat and trapped tension before. Shifts we make in visible surroundings may look like they are happening because the weather is good for construction, or the funding has finally been secured—but they can also, perhaps always, be read as reflections of an interior shift, a changing mind. People don't get stuck in houses, they get stuck in their imagination of partnership.

Housing and life-style markets at the end of the 20th century continue to urge a stupefying conformity that puts a curse on marriage and partnerships of all kinds. Fortunately, there are architects and dreamers who prevail in pushing the limits imposed by the stereotyped, boxed version of relationship. These artists-of-dwelling succeed in creating spaces for us to imaginatively house ourselves with room for intimacy.

The kind of intimacy meant here is not necessarily between people. Gaston Bachelard wrote his entire primer on intimacy (*Poetics of Space*) without once mentioning the space between people. Prior to conceiving of intimacy between human beings, the phenomenologist explores the lost world of things that constitutes intimate space. Intimacy simply makes that which is "inmost" available. A dwelling with intimate spaces is a dwelling capable of dreaming. It has avenues into the interior that invite thought about what goes on beneath the surface. Such a house is alive. It radiates a story, has its own eros. It gathers images to itself and fabricates a reality out of what it has been given. Stepping into such a space, when it suits your particular requirements for interiority, is experienced as a pleasant seduction.

When asked, people tend to know what they require for accessing what is "inmost." Sometimes it is simply a well-placed wall. C. G. Jung, who writes luxurious descriptions of what attracts the soul, needed a blank wall in front of his desk in order to focus the thoughts that mattered. HD burned pinecones on a square table in her room on the Zürichsee. Simone de Beauvoir ecstatically plastered her single room at the back of her grandmother's boarding-house with orange wallpaper. "Uniqueness is the signature of intimate space," says Bachelard, recalling his childhood pantry; it is the smell of raisins drying on a wicker tray that leads him back to the image. Sensual details are held within the architectural elements that attract our memories. I know a woman who built an elegant Chinese lacquer-floored room for doing Tai Chi, and a man who constructed a raised, floor-to-ceiling glass-paned room so he could visually track passing thunderstorms. They both drew plans with an awareness of how architectural elements can extend the soul's radius, pushing the reach of their own desire into the house that holds them. Of course the area of imaginal design becomes quite complicated when taking the needs of two or more individuals into account. I, for example, was married to the storm-tracker, and dreamed that the upper story he was constructing for himself was a black metal box, like a prison, for me.

A couple's house should be made up of two kinds of places, the shared couple's realm and the individual private worlds. The shared realm should be half-public and half-intimate. The individual worlds should be entirely private.

The architect Christopher Alexander's design design is an attempt at resolving the age-old Njord-Skadi dilemma in Scandinavian mythology where Njord loved the sea and Skadi the mountains. Each was restless and ill at ease in the place of the other so they established a festival of meeting in between.

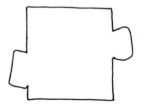

Addressing the delicate problem of the balance of solitudes, Alexander suggests that its resolution requires the couple's extension of itself into the world—into close, neighborly, and family-like contact with other adults. Then, when one needs privacy, the other has possibilities for companionship at hand. But how large a field is required for companionship? And how much privacy is required for solitude? May Sarton indirectly addresses these issues in her story about seeing two people on a distant beach. When the two figures are seen as fishermen the scene is idyllic. If the figures are seen as poets, it is disturbing because "there is one solitude too many."

One of the designs I have lived expands Alexander's couple plan in space and time to include a roving shared realm anchored by separate private dwellings. There is his place, and my place, and the places in the world where we meet.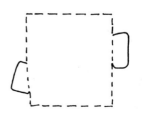

Living in distinct dwellings makes it necessary to be taken into each other's intimacy. Such a design asks me to consider how my house houses him, and how his house houses me. The arrangement is stable, but with an added note of impermanence because of the ever-present question, "Will you live together some day?" Such existential impermanence is highly recommended by the dreamer of spaces (Bachelard) who considers the finality of living in a "dream house" to be a sort of death and wants to keep "the dream of a house we will live in sometime" delayed, for so long that there will never be time to achieve it.

This advice is in keeping with the architect's who says, do not build a dream house from scratch. Because the house plays such a critical role in relationship—bringing out conflict, offering the chance of resolution—there must always be room for rearranging, improving, enlarging, fixing up, tearing down, changing. For the oneiric architect (the dreaming one), the challenge is to design domains of intimacy rather than to construct close quarters. Intimacy is never repellent, unlike closeness.

Some examples follow, many of them from artists. Not necessarily because they have the solutions, but because they have no personal life, as Diane Di Prima once said, and their experimental designs for housing relationships make news.

John Guare (playwright, *Six Degrees of Separation*) and Adele Chatfield-Taylor have apartments that share the same service hall. When they got married her mother asked, "Well, now are you going to live together?" The reply: "Certainly not! Why let a little thing like matrimony ruin a big thing like good design?"

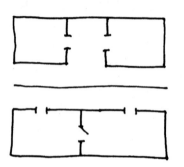

And a composer and opera singer in Madrid have side-by-side units with an adjoining door that locks on her side.

Sarah Delano Roosevelt's mother-in-law solution was anathema to intimacy. Her wedding gift to her son Franklin and his new bride, Eleanor, when they returned from their honeymoon trip to Europe, was a brownstone in New York. Not only did she completely decorate the new home for them, but she also purchased the brownstone next door for herself and had doors installed on each of the five floors so she could walk into their space any time.

With regard to changing and re-arranging a marriage dwelling according to the necessity of its partners, in this case mutable, affectional and artistic necessities, the relationship of Vita Sackville-West and Harold Nicholson provides two unique models. Their situation requires the special mention of certain elements in the Architecture of Intimacy that need chapters of their own: the garden and the tower.

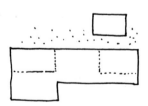

At Long Barn they had separate wings with separate bedrooms. The children had their own house behind the back garden.

At Sissinghurst they shared a house together but had separate bedrooms. Each person in the family had his or her own sitting-room, and Vita had a tower. Different colored gardens covered the grounds between their individual spaces.

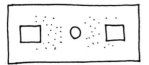

Their garden was an image of their marriage. Harold designed and Vita planted. His classical hand set the urns and placed the paths. Her romantic touch directed the overflowing vines (clematis, figs, wisteria) and chose the wild colors. This plotting and blossoming was their shared realm, where (according to their observant son) permanence and mutation wed.

But the space with the most interiority remained private. Vita's tower admitted very few. Even the children had to call to her from the steps below. "The tower has a vaulted ceiling which is a great principle of intimacy for it constantly reflects intimacy at its center." (Bachelard) The first floor of her tower is a serene, adobe pink sitting-room. The second floor is her study. At the end of her study, the room curls into a round library that took my breath away. It is so small that you can stand in the center and reach the books all around in a perfect circle. Walking into it opened a surprising space in my imagination—a little, virginal space I remembered in connection to the Mouseketeer Annette Funicello on a round bed pictured in *Seventeen* magazine thirty-five years ago. A round bed suggests curling up with oneself in the tremendous adventure of longing—in those days it meant reading and dreaming and talking on the phone with girlfriends in the same circle.

A tower is private, magical, and productive of fantasy. One of the best second generation *Babar the Elephant* books is about the Old Lady writing a book in a tower. Pom and Flora hoist food up to her ever day in a little straw basket on a pulley system. I learned in recent years that the man who wrote this book married Phyllis Rose, author of *Parallel Lives* and astute observer of intricate Victorian marriage arrangements among literary couples. DeBrunhoff and Rose apparently live in separate houses with separate studies to house their different libraries.

These ideas don't really require trust funds to implement. A friend of mine has a way of going into her own tower place by changing a colored cap for her children. The littlest one knows that when her mother is at the desk wearing her red cap, she is not supposed to interrupt, but when she is wearing the blue cap she'll talk as much as she wants. Her technique is a version of Carl Jung's habit while in residence at his tower in Bollingen: to raise mood flags on a pole to alert friends and neighbors. One color meant "stay away" and another, "come ahead."

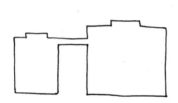

Another critical element of imaginal architecture is the bridge. Frida Kahlo had a small blue house (Casa Chica) and Diego Rivera a large pink one (Casa Grande) joined at the top. Their design raises the question: at what level is your relationship joined?

Through the garage, the level of techne, where tools and cars are stored. This is the place of implements for entering into and interacting with the environs.

Through the kitchen, where the table collects us, alone, with family, with company. A place of public restoration, food preparation, where news of the day is spread and read and talked over.

Through the bedroom, the space made intimate by our private belongings. Where we remove clothed personae, lie under comforters, seclude our dreambooks, cradle our heads, fantasize, live the body's erotic pleasures.

Through the study/studio, where we practice our art, craft our words, wonder, reflect, fabricate. Where we re-create ourselves. The place of good light, gathered resources, bookshelves, large waste-baskets.

A third floor bridge and terrace system connected Diego's Casa Grande and Frida's Casa Chica. Connecting through at this level means having soul-work in common. A place where there are shared images, bridged by a language of your own.

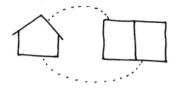

There are both positive and negative links through creative work: Yves Tanguay and Kay Sage had a connection through their studios in a converted barn behind their house. They lived together, but worked in creative spaces divided by a solid wall. They never knew (and did not discuss) what the other was working on.

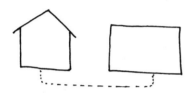

Vanessa Bell shared a house with Clive Bell and their children. The youngest child was Duncan Grant's. She lived with Grant during the day at their Charleston house studio.

Virginia Woolf called the studio "the masterpiece and joint memorial to their left-handed marriage." (A left-handed marriage is traditionally one in which there is no property, and no children, no possessing rings exchanged. The man simply takes the woman's hand in his left hand to signify their agreement. Usually it would be a bad position for the woman to be in, but Vanessa Bell redefines tradition.)

Women gave another twist to the ideal of marriage at the end of the nineteenth century by forming unions called, in New England, Boston marriages. Alice James, sister of William and Henry, lived in such an arrangement at the end of her life. As did the novelist Sarah Orne Jewett and her friend Annie Field after her husband (editor of the *Atlantic Monthly*) died. They were together for thirty years then, sharing a house in Boston for seven months, then separating for five when Sarah would retreat to South Berwick, Maine to write. They traveled to Europe together frequently, and had a social life of friends in common including the young Willa Cather who went on to live in such a union with another woman for forty years (Faderman). I don't know how Cather and her friend arranged their housing.

One hundred years ago, Edward Carpenter, who was a friend of experimentation between the sexes, wrote about the delusional housing of set-apart relationships: "...by a kind of absurd fiction, marriage is represented as an oasis situated in the midst of an arid desert, in which it is pretended that neither of the two parties is so fortunate as to find any object of interest in the desert surround."

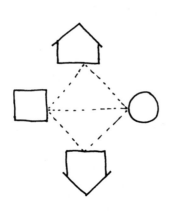

In this example, the two central parties found other objects of interest to support their bond of passion. Henry Murray and Christiana Morgan, each in on-going marriages, constructed an intricate pattern over the course of many years. They maintained separate dwellings with their respective spouses, but worked together at an institute in Cambridge, and shared a tryst place in her singular tower.

"The marriage of the future is always a ruin of the marriage of the present."
—Carpenter

Separate spaces posit triangles. There is my place, your place, and the place where we meet. Whether or not the triangle involves a third person, a third space destabilizes a potentially stagnant twoness and generates movement.

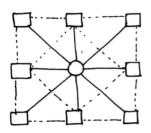

The desire behind this design was literalized in the sixties' ideal of communal life (for example, Peter Rabbit's commune in Colorado) where everyone lived in separate dwellings linked by a communal hearth.

But the variations are endless and a pattern of withdrawal and emergence into and out of the presence of others also occurs in single dwellings that structurally recognize difference.

Writer and painter, Robert Duncan and his partner Jess shared a three story house with a library on the bottom, shared space in the middle, and Jess's studio at the top.

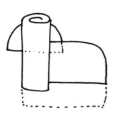

A composer and an actor in Spain built a house with a mandala-capped tower that spirals up from his theater in the basement past her music studio on the second floor. They each have their own bedroom, as do their children.

Houses for more than one person need to have structures to enable separation: walls, long work tables, different levels, deep yards, upstairs outside porches, discrete lighting (reading lights for one), solid doors, and window seats. And elements that encourage touching: couches for two, softening colors, beds, small passage ways between some rooms, intimate tables for eating, entryways to facilitate greetings.

"In a palace there is no place for intimacy."
—Baudelaire

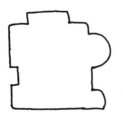

Houses for one person require an intensity of designed space, rather than dispersion. A central space with alcoves surrounding.

A writer who is mistress of the single dwelling describes the experience of falling in love with the rich habitation of another person. How is it that we can walk into another's space and instantly know we are "at home?" The room has a special tone, a hidden music, "it reverberated with oceans and tides and waves of the owner's past...the essence of human life as it has lived into certain colors, objets d'art, and ...books...The longing is to be taken into that world by what the French call an *amitie amoureuse*, recognized from the start as an attraction...a soul-affinity." "The value of life lived alone (is) that it is lived in a house with an open door...with room for the stranger, and for the new friend to be taken in and cherished." (May Sarton)

These designs are about how the space between people takes shape:

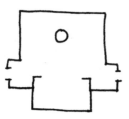

Two friends in Minnesota who both like to cook built two kitchens on either side of the family room. One for her and one for him. Their conversation can have two distinct sources of heat, and a shared game table in the background.

A relationship with inherent separateness can share the same living room and source of heat. Leopold Stokowski's horseshoe-shaped house in the hills of Montecito around a central pool has doors between each chamber and fireplaces in each dividing wall. The special room constructed for Greta Garbo has a lock on her side of the door and a private garden in the back.

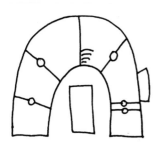

There is little hope for intimacy in a relationship where the requirements for nourishing the imaginal life of another are ignored, misunderstood, or taken lightly. The blueprints imposed on relationships in adult life are limited and limiting.

"With regard to marriage, we need more complex plots."
—Phyllis Rose

It is necessary to inquire after one another's idiosyncratic needs for intimacy—with things. This is the province of the Erotes painted in action on ancient Greek vases: tiny winged creatures attend to the aesthetic details of the space between people. They set flowers on a table, hold up a mirror to reflect the beauty in a room, provide pools of water to refresh tired travelers. Any design for a dwelling that retains its dreaming—in any relationship that wants a future or for the future of marriage—needs to provide windows for those winged impulses.

A last word about gossip. It should be a required moral duty— necessary for good citizenship—to talk about marriage. "It is as important to talk about marriages as it is to talk about the national election." (Rose) People are desperate to know how other people manage their lives. Biography sections in bookstores are growing exponentially. It is freeing to tell these stories. It helps our exhausted fantasy life to picture Mr. and Mrs. Blake sitting naked together in the quiet garden behind their house, or to imagine Mr. and Mrs. Yeats engaged in automatic trance writing in a train compartment traveling through the Celtic countryside. Anecdotes of this quality are antidotes, just as my houseplans intend, to the dulled collective imagination of intimacy and modern partnership.

References

Alexander, Christopher. *A Pattern Language*. New York: Oxford UP, 1977.

Bachelard, Gaston. *Poetics of Space*. Boston: Beacon Press, 1969.

Carpenter, Edward. *Love's Coming of Age*. New York: Boni and Liverwright, 1911.

Chadwick, Whitney and Isabelle de Courtivron. *Significant Others*. London: Thames and Hudson, 1993.

Faderman, Lillian. *Surpassing the Love of Men*. New York: William Morrow, 1981.

Nicolson, Nigel. *Portrait of a Marriage*. New York: Atheneum, 1980.

Rose, Phyllis. *Parallel Lives*. New York: Vintage, 1984.

Sarton, May. *Journal of a Solitude*. New York: W. W. Norton, 1973.

"MARRIAGE IS IMPOSSIBLE!"
SCATTERED THOUGHTS OF A MARRIED MAN

JOSEPH J. LANDRY

B etween the two of us, we had been married four times. Over lunch he said simply, "Marriage is impossible!" I knew immediately what he meant. Marriage is an impossible topic—maybe *the* impossible topic. Just try to put into words what makes a friend's marriage work, never mind your own. It's impossible to fully describe, predict, or to arrive at a consensus. Marriage is one of those subjects sure to disrupt conversation at most dinner parties. It is one of the ultimate products of the human imagination, appearing in countless forms and varieties. Everybody's had at it: all sorts of reformers and feminists for whom marriage presents itself as oppression, legalized rape, etc., contrasted lately by the right wing (Christian, Muslim and otherwise) who see each heterosexual marriage as an act of salvation for civilization.

Why get married, anyway? Societal reasons for matrimony no longer seem to ring true. You don't need vows or civil ceremonies to set up housekeeping. You can live with anyone you like. Children are produced without fear of the taint of illegitimacy and, given the current fertilization methods available, seemingly without husbands. And with the present rates of divorce, no ar-

Joseph J. Landry is a hairdresser in Worcester, Massachusetts. He is married, happily.

gument that sanctifies the stability provided by marriage seems to hold up. Offer the same people who say that marriage is a stabilizing force the chance to invest in a company which has a fifty-fifty chance of going out of business and "stable" would be the last word they would use to describe the venture. Yet we marry over and over. Why? It's not logical and it defies reason.

Getting married is like joining the Mafia. I don't mean to imply anything criminal (since you end up as an in-law rather than an outlaw), nor do I wish to contrast the gang oaths with the "unto death do you part" stuff. No, what I mean to get at is the idea that when you marry, you join something bigger than yourself and your partner. And you don't get this if you merely live together. In cohabitation, one plus one equals two. To be married is to be in a triad: you, me and "the marriage."

If we "meet at the altar," we meet in the imagination, at the archetype. With the altar comes sacrifice and offering, and with that a God or Gods, and further with Gods come fantasies, perspectives and enshrined precincts. The point of getting married is to pay tribute to the marriage Gods. This act, similar to pledging loyalty to the Godfather, seeks to ensure that on the days when ill fortune invades the marriage some sort of circle of protection has been drawn around the relationship. You are on the Godfather's turf. But remember that this Godfather of marriage may one day ask you to do a favor: you may have to sacrifice something for the marriage.

"Marriage is impossible" because it is archetypal. Married people develop a relationship not only with each other but with their idea, their fantasy of marriage not unlike the relationship of artist to the muse. "How will this affect the marriage?" married people ask themselves. "Marriage is impossible" because it's an art. And in this art is the attempt at bringing the living mythic image into the flesh, be that image Hera and Zeus, Mary and Joseph, Abraham and Sarah, or Ozzie and Harriet. Perhaps marriage is the ultimate performance art.

And speaking of performance, one common complaint about marriage is that the sexual passion unleashed during dating is often sacrificed at the altar. The remarks of another friend illustrate the single man's dread of this phenomenon. After congratulating me on my recent marriage, my friend asked how long ago my wife and I had wed. When I responded "six months," he asked, "So...did you stop fucking yet?"

What my friend feared is the unnamed conversion that takes place somewhere between the single and married states. I think that this conversion can be best understood by inventing two new archetypal models derived from human evolution: the hunter-gatherer and the farmer-cultivator.

The truly single people are best described as the hunter-gatherers. They know that the game shifts to different grazing areas constantly and that today's bright berries wither on the bush at the next morning's light. They're on the move, they play the field, they can't be tied down. They don't call, they don't write. The hunter-gatherers are big fans of display: they're masters at the art of Aphroditic attraction. An old married friend (who, I suspect, missed the hunt) used to call women's perfume "buck lure." Some of the hunters go on and on, and never marry. Others undergo a transformation and become a "good catch."

The marrying kind bear the farmer-cultivator archetype. They tend to seed a single field, store grain for the lean times, seek to understand the cyclical nature of things, are masters of delayed gratification. To assign animal totems to each group, imagine the single hunter-gatherer types as wild, roaming creatures, while the animals representing the married farmer-cultivator types are "domesticated."

The sexual style of the hunter-gatherer is illustrated daily on television nature shows: the animal's nose to the air on the scent, in an indiscriminate rut, seeking God knows what with God knows whom, and God knows how. The farmer-cultivator's sexual style is depicted by the twin oxen "hitched" to the plowing yoke: gone is the head to head charge of sexual attraction that drives the singles. Instead, the marrieds sublimate some of the sex energy to "pulling the plow," the day to day tasks that constitute "working on the marriage." At night they fall exhausted into the barn, and do whatever they have energy left to do. They're not "opposites attracting," à la Romeo and Juliet. They're more like siblings—Egyptian royal brother and sister ruling together over the kingdom.

If all this sounds as if the hunter-gatherers have it better, be assured that many of them go days, weeks, months, even years without finding what they're looking for. And in further favor of the farmer-cultivator types, what appears to be a vacuum left by the departing sexual fury is soon filled with other delights, unavailable to the wanderer.

One final crazy idea: make all marriage licenses expire after five to seven years. Instead of going to court to get divorced, make couples who wish to remain married go to court to present their case for marriage license renewal. Eliminate divorce lawyers in favor of barristers who can clearly articulate the mystery of each matrimonial case.

Imagine proceedings under this new form of jurisprudence (erotic law): testimony from both husband and wife, children, relatives, mothers and fathers-in-law could be submitted; teachers, coaches, Boy and Girl Scout leaders could provide the court with the children's report cards, science projects, Little League participation etc., as a measure of the family's success. And not least of all, attorneys could get depositions from all in the community who act to support the marriage. Maybe all who were present during the wedding could be re-invited.

People in cities and towns after all support the arts now by turning out for plays, concerts and exhibitions. In keeping with such community support for the arts, why not a public forum for the regular appreciation of those who continue to attempt the impossible?

REALISM
AND THE ARCHETYPES:
DAISY MILLER

NANCY TENFELDE CLASBY

R ealism and myth study differ so widely in their premises
and focus that archetypal analysis is seldom applied to
realistic fiction. The "air of reality," the "solidity of
specification," Henry James described in *The Art of Fiction* is often seen as a reaction against the mythic archetypes of romantic
literature. The prosaic surface of realistic stories appears to pre-
clude the color and play of fantasy popularly associated with
myth. If we examine the narrative structures underlying realist
fiction, however, we find the archetypal patterns of the hero
myth. The divergence between the authorized sociological
framework laid down by realist theory and the mythic patterns
actually deployed in its texts generates a tension peculiar to realist
fiction. In that dissonance lies the source of realism's power to
evoke the dark emotions of bewilderment and despair.

In addition to being a reaction against myth and romanticism,
realism was an effort to validate imaginative literature by providing it with a science-based theoretical structure. Realism promised
"a slice of life," a faithful *mimesis*, based on careful observation, of

Nancy Clasby, Ph.D., is a Lecturer in English at the University of Miami, Coral Gables, Florida. She is currently working on a book on images of the sacred in American literature.

typical social interactions. It would hold up the mirror to a society functioning on Darwinian principles of survival of the fittest. It would demonstrate the deterministic pressures of heredity and environment. While realist novels were made to mirror the ambient social conventions, they were often critical of the power structure they reflected. Henry James, for example, wished to portray an oppressive society, while insisting on "respect for the liberty" of his characters. He conceived of his creations as emerging in a sort of natural or organic development, untouched by authorial manipulation (Seltzer 88). He sought "freedom" for his characters and disavowed the "crime of power," but as a realist he worked within the parameters of determinism and the other restrictive forces predicated by the social sciences of his day. The "liberty" envisioned by the artist is the capacity for self-realization through action exemplified in the mythic archetypes. But the dynamics of realism do not allow for heroic development; they move the narrative in a "relentlessly coherent, determined, and 'genetic' progress, always in a direction preestablished, from unhappy childhood to unhappy marriage..." to a conclusion in isolation and rather prosaic failure (Seltzer 172). Even in the hands of so resolute a critic of the "forces of the money power" as James, realist fiction replicates and thus implicitly ratifies the economic and social determinism it mirrors.[1]

Realism, then, involves a double project: it seeks to authenticate imaginative literature by making it reflect the views of the social sciences, and at the same time it sets up a separate aesthetic base as a platform for criticizing the power drive of a technologically based social order. It seeks to safeguard and even dignify *poesis* by cultivating a mystique of "objectivity" and detached reportage,

---

[1]Although Henry James retained a degree of optimistic belief in the power of virtue to affect fate, it is fair, I think, to say that the underlying momentum of realism pulled his work toward determinism, emphasizing the power of the social environment. Daniel Mark Fogel's *Henry James and the Structure of the Romantic Imagination* (Baton Rouge: Louisiana State University Press, 1981) suggests that James turns in his late novels to the romantic archetype. M. H. Abrams (*Natural Supernaturalism.* Norton, 1971) calls the "spiral return." Milly Theale in *The Wings of the Dove*, for example, enacts the mythic trope of death and rebirth in her forgiveness of those who have wronged her.

but contradictory yearnings for "freedom" lurk beneath the stoic, no-nonsense narratives, threatening the correct surfaces.

The novelist's apparently disinterested accuracy of reportage calls for a similarly objective observational stance on the reader's part. The writer's task is to train the reader in objectivity and detachment. An ideal reader learns to concede that failure is "sad but inevitable," and assumes the role of observer, refraining from judgment. But the mythic substructures are at odds with this surface agenda and draw the reader to reject the inevitability of failure. The archetypal elements in the narrative often carry the burden of expressing the writer's own unresolved relationship to the power structure. They also invite the reader to move past the narrative's nominally value-free objectivity and to assess the moral integrity of the protagonists.

All the sad young men, the anti-heroes like James's Frederick Winterbourne, Hemingway's Jake Barnes, and Nick Carraway of *The Great Gatsby*, are the chief figures and the products of the realist tradition—subjects doomed by theory to fail. Insofar as realism offers a counter-myth to the heroic journey it may be that of Frankenstein's monster, the hero as a faulty product of science, animated but not fully realized, cold, potentially destructive, and pitiable. As a genre, realism seeks to project an unassailably objective picture of the so-called real world. When viewed from the perspective of the archetypes it presents a nightmarish fantasy of the self reduced to automaton.

Realist protagonists are doomed to struggle against the dragon that is society itself—the power structure envisioned in the social science terms adopted by realism. Occasionally rogues, or madmen, or innocents function as protagonists, providing focal points for the picaresque plots and ironic detachment so typical of the genre. If one of these rogue/innocents ends successfully, like Dreiser's Sister Carrie, it is with the rueful message that blind luck plays a part in a deterministic world. Rarely, a Huck Finn or a Jay Gatsby chooses his fate: Huck risks himself to save Jim, saying "All right, then, I'll *go* to hell." Gatsby dies in misplaced allegiance to his dream. Milly Theale in *The Wings of the Dove* preserves her integrity and even prevails, spreading her protective wings over those she loves. But more typically, the hero *manqué* appears unwilling to engage in struggle with the dragon, unable even to grasp the terms of such a conflict. He is stalled in the wasteland where the myth of heroic quest begins, never *in medias res*, but perpetually in the ante-chamber. Images of aimless circling so common in realist fiction represent the hero's inability to set a course and so pass through the outer margins of experience into life's arena.

The baffled pity evoked by realist fiction is based less on the clearly visualized circumstances of the characters' lives than on the unformulated sense of something missing or not achieved. Deconstructionists are fond of pointing to the *aporia* or subversive absences undercutting conscious levels of discourse. Archetypal myth underlies realist fiction not as an absence, but as an unseen presence. It is almost invisible but it exerts a gravitational pull, tugging at the narrative like a dark moon over tidal waters. A good illustration of the submerged tensions created by mythic paradigms in realist fiction is Henry James's *Daisy Miller*.

This novel is, as Daniel Mark Fogel says, a "dark comedy of manners" played out in the continental resorts of the 1870's.[2] James traces, in precise detail, the social interactions of his two young and wealthy American characters, Daisy and Winterbourne. The outcome, Daisy's death, has been variously attributed to misunderstandings, cultural determinism or the corruption of European society. Some critics fault Daisy for having "no sense of the inevitable...[of] traditions and taboos..." (Dupee 94). Others blame the outcome on Frederick Winterbourne's "low emotional temperature" (Fogel 44). In keeping with realism's detached, objective stance, most critics seek a balanced distribution of responsibility for the catastrophe. Realism posits a diminished level of responsibility in a deterministic world, and so promotes non-judgmental observation. Myth deals in moral discernment calling for judgment, upsetting the balanced equation of blame.

---

[2]Fogel and a number of other critics prefer the original version of *Daisy Miller* over James's 1909 New York revision. Fogel feels that the later version "poeticizes" Daisy and gives her moral ascendancy over Winterbourne (94-95). I have used the 1909 text except where indicated. The mythic pattern I have traced is implicit in both versions and the differences in the text, though interesting, are peripheral to my point.

Seen from the mythic perspective, *Daisy Miller* begins in what appears to be an Edenic garden where Russian princesses and American heiresses dance in rustling muslin. Vevey in the sunshine appears vibrant with life and color. The first clues that this fairytale landscape may conceal a darker stratum emerge when the narrative focuses on Winterbourne, a young American gentleman idling in the garden on a summer morning. His friends, we learn, describe him as a student in Geneva. His enemies, "but after all he had no enemies," suggest that he remains in Geneva because of an involvement with "a lady who lived there—a foreign lady, a person older than himself" (4). Winterbourne, twenty-seven, is in Vevey dancing attendance upon his wealthy aunt, Mrs. Costello. He is "at liberty" this morning only because she has taken to her bed with a headache. As he looks at the young women, the "graceful objects" moving about him, he is accosted by Randolph Miller, an American "urchin of nine or ten" with sharp little features, red stockings and tie and a pointed walking stick he pokes into the flower beds and even into the trains of the ladies' dresses.

Randolph precedes his sister, functioning as a sort of trickster figure, or shadow for the beautiful Daisy. All his unruliness, his boisterous intractability, his determined Americanism prefigure his sister's more refined vitality. Daisy appears in glowing white, resplendent in "frills and flounces and knots of pale-colored ribbon" (8). She has "the *tournure* of a princess."[3] "How pretty they are!" thinks Winterbourne, condescending in his choice of adjective and in his categorization of Daisy as one of a larger class of "American girls."

Knowing that he would not be "at liberty" in Geneva to speak to such a young woman, Winterbourne advances at once to his encounter with Daisy. After his first remarks, he fears that he may have been too precipitous, but resolves to "gallantly advance rather than retreat" (9). The martial imagery complements the development of the archetypal pattern of the princess and the knight errant, but also suggests the dangerous ambiguities of Winterbourne's stance toward Daisy. He is charmed and drawn to the

---

[3] The quote is from the first edition of the novel.

young woman, but he is also puzzled. She seems to him composed of "charming little parts that didn't match and that made no *ensemble*..." Neither bold nor insipid, "her expression was as decently limpid as the very cleanest water." He concludes "very forgivingly," that she is in "want of finish"(11). She must "have no idea whatever of 'form.'" Charmed, "amused and perplexed," Winterbourne cannot find a formula to define Daisy.

He wonders if he has "lived at Geneva so long as to have got morally muddled" (16). Has he "lost the right sense for the young American tone[?]" He asks if she is an innocent or a "designing, an audacious...an expert young person." Winterbourne's initial conclusion is that Daisy is not a European "coquette," but "only a pretty American flirt." For her part, Daisy remarks that Winterbourne does not seem to her like an American. The muddled perceptions warn that the garden at Vevey is not what it seems. It is a labyrinth, and the hero will be called upon to rescue the princess from its confines.

The minotaur in the labyrinth appears in the person of Winterbourne's aunt, Mrs. Costello. A "widow of fortune," she instructs her nephew in "the minutely hierarchical constitution" (23) of New York society. The Millers are, she informs him, "horribly common" and of "the last crudity." Mrs. Costello refuses to be introduced to Daisy and warns Winterbourne away from her. "You've lived too long out of the country. You'll be sure to make some great mistake" (26).

Mrs. Costello represents a class of matriarchs, wealthy, "vigilant matrons who massed themselves in the forefront of social intercourse in the dark old city at the other end of the lake" (35). They control the marriages of their offspring, assuring that their alliances bring social and economic advantage. In effect, they imprison the princess in the maze until their price has been paid or until they are successfully challenged. For all the elegance and refinement of Vevey, the drive to control and expand wealth is the driving force in social exchange. In *English Hours* James described this phenomenon as "the steady rumble of that deep keynote of English manners, overscored so often, and with such sweet beguilements, by finer harmonies, but never extinguished—the economic struggle for existence." In mythic terms, the matrons are the dragons in the wasteland. Winterbourne is quite aware that "given certain circumstances," he could "see himself afraid—literally afraid—of these ladies" (75).

To a large extent, Winterbourne's dilemma is based on a conflict between two mutually contradictory "languages." Mrs. Costello and the other women speak a limited but imperative dialect familiar to Winterbourne in all its nuances. It is a proclamatory language seeking to capture Daisy in a "barrage of would-be definitive epithets" (Graham 52): "a dreadful girl," "very common," "hopelessly vulgar." Daisy, however, eludes their linear categories, remaining alternately baffling and disconcertingly direct. She is often concealed behind a parasol or a fan, only to reappear, center stage, leading Winterbourne in a dance of advance and retreat. She is described again and again as "going on," "going round,' "going too far" (Weisbuch 65). Though Winterbourne sometimes advances, sometimes follows her lead, he "can't dance," and is often seen vacillating or in retreat. Some of Daisy's apparently pointless chatter about her putative engagement is also dance-like, a sort of ceremonial speech, a riddle, part of the ritual testing of the hero. It is important not in itself but in the reaction it provokes in Winterbourne. James builds a network of images of scrutiny, appearances and interpretation, tracing Winterbourne's efforts to respond to Daisy's ritual speech in the face of the commanding instructions of his society.

Mark Seltzer's study of power in Henry James's work points out that the social circles James described functioned as self-regulating social hierarchies. Deterrents and even punishment within this system need not be overt since the participants are thoroughly socialized, responsive to hints and innuendoes. Surveillance of even the most commonplace interchange is the means of enforcing restraint. In *Daisy Miller* the overseeing matrons enforce the delicately balanced mechanics of self-policing by scrutinizing Daisy and Winterbourne's every gesture.

Daisy is wealthy and she "dresses in perfection" (23) so she is initially, provisionally, "recognized" by Mrs. Walker and some others of the international set. Images of "appearances" dominate the scene in the Pincean Garden where Daisy defies the system by "exhibiting herself" (54) with her Italian suitor, Giovanelli. "Fifty people have remarked her," says Mrs. Walker, as she tries to draw Daisy into her carriage, "so that the world may see she's not running absolutely wild" (59). At first Winterbourne objects to Mrs. Walker's efforts at coercion, but soon he succumbs to her imperatives, abandoning Daisy. As he looks back at her, she is obscured behind a parasol, outside his field of vision.

Daisy does not respond to social scrutiny nor does she accept definition in society's terms. She tells Mrs. Walker, "I don't think I want to know what you mean" (62). The demands of "appearances" are a foreign language to the young woman. When she resists, she makes herself unreadable within the framework of society's language. In the system of restraints based on observation, inscrutability is intolerable. Daisy loses her significance, her power to mean, and so begins the progression from "objectification," being talked about, to being "cut dead," eliminated from the system of signification.

For all the refinements of communication represented by the Europeanized Americans, the limitations and rigidities of their language are clear. Winterbourne, for example, attempts to defend Daisy to his aunt by distinguishing between innocence, ignorance and moral evil. Mrs. Costello refuses to be drawn into these "question[s] for the metaphysicians" (46), and dismisses further interpretation by categorizing the Millers as "hopelessly vulgar." "For this short life," she says, "that's quite enough." She concludes that Daisy "thinks of nothing at all. She romps on from day to day, from hour to hour, as they did in the Golden Age. I can imagine nothing more vulgar" (77). The narrow limits of Mrs. Costello's interpretive field do not extend to simple distinctions between innocence and moral guilt, much less to the complexities of freedom and expanded vision Daisy promises.

Winterbourne himself lives on several levels of appearance. On the surface he is an irreproachable, good-natured young gentleman fully attuned to the demands of his society. On another less public level he indulges in the (permitted) vice of dalliance with an older, foreign woman. As Robert Weisbuch points out, Winterbourne's hidden self is "pornographic and musty,"

[He] associates the libido with the hidden---that is why he despises meeting Daisy in the hotel hall (not simply because it is vaguely vulgar) and it is why, once they arrive at Chillon, he bribes the custodian to leave them alone...It is also why he cannot believe in Daisy's appearance of innocence, because his own appearance is so unnaturally fashioned to disguise what resides in Geneva and himself (78).

In spite of Winterbourne's alliance with the dragon, his role as hero indicates that he must be understood as possessing at least the potential for choosing Daisy. His generalized fear of powerful women may indicate a deeper fear of the ultimate loss of "instinct" and vitality represented by Daisy. Though he is capable of understanding her true role, Daisy remains for him "an inscrutable combination of audacity and innocence" (59).

Realist fiction seeks to present an accurate reflection of ordinary lives, a detached, disinterested portrait. It calls upon the reader not to judge, but to observe. Still, critics do ask "Who is to blame for Daisy's death?" Of the many possible interpretations, the most common is that the disaster was mutually produced. Neither character "can overcome the environmental determinism that finally makes it impossible for Daisy and Winterbourne to meet each other halfway, she by growing beyond the crude provinciality of Schenectady and he by growing beyond the stifling proprieties of Geneva and of the American colony in Rome" (Fogel 97). The realist bent toward objectivity inspires a self-consciously evenhanded judgment.

But the mythic elements underlying the narrative upset the neat balance of blame. Seen as hero and princess, the characters have certain inviolable roles to play. Both figures are highly charged, set aside from the relatively lifeless background figures. Like Randolph, who precedes Daisy, their personal energies are at variance with the currents of society. The boy, as trickster, is a center of random disturbance. Daisy and Winterbourne depart from social standards in a more purposeful way. Something of the outlaw clings to the heroic figure. The princess, as imperiled heroine, challenges the wicked stepmother and rushes in where angels fear to tread. The hero may be forgiven awkwardness, any number of mistakes, and even occasional failures of nerve as long as he persists in his mission. If both willingly enact their roles the drama ends in the royal marriage, signifying full individuation. The prince is not permitted to refuse to espouse the princess; a final rejection signals a profound violation of his own role. Winterbourne's failure to engage in single-hearted struggle for Daisy's hand brings him into collusion with society in bringing about her death.

As long as Winterbourne remains Daisy's defender, their sometimes confused, apparently contradictory gestures remain essentially harmonious. When Winterbourne slips from his mythic role into the arena of realism, a shift occurs in the alignment of the two opposing figures, the prince and the princess. The dualist codes shaping Winterbourne's society cannot accommodate the dance of mythic opposites. When he rejects the shades and ambiguities of their relationship, reducing Daisy's meaning to "a mere black little blot," Winterbourne adopts the imperial language of the power structure. The oppositions set up by the Darwinian code can be resolved only by the destruction of the weaker member. The erstwhile prince becomes the agent of Daisy's destruction.

Early in their relationship, Winterbourne shows himself capable of playing his mythic role. Shortly after Daisy and Winterbourne meet, she agrees to go with him on a trip to the Castle of Chillon. This forbidden venture reveals Winterbourne's capacity to challenge society's limits. He is, of course, anxious about appearances, but Daisy enters, tripping down the stairs, "dressed exactly in the way that consorted best, to his fancy, with their adventure" (39). The "delightfully irregular" moment encourages his fantasy that they are "*really* going 'off'" together. As they sail to the castle he remarks, significantly, that he "was never better pleased" in his life. The moment of defiant adherence to the princess provides him with a thrilling sense of "some small sweet strain of romance, not intense but clear and sweet" (39).

But even in this scene, Winterbourne's fatal inadequacy is prefigured by Daisy's question, "What on earth are you so grave[4] about?...You look as if you were taking me to a prayer-meeting or a funeral" (40). Many details, beginning with the names of the characters, point to the outcome of their relationship. "Daisy" is a common wildflower, linked to the sun (day's eye); "Winterbourne" suggests the killing cold season. Though deeply drawn to Daisy, Winterbourne also wants to be rid of her and safe from the challenge she presents. It would "simplify the solution," he thinks, if he could dismiss her as a victim of "lawless passions" (59).

The scene at Mrs. Walker's party where the hostess "cuts Daisy dead," prefigures the final scene in the Colosseum. When Mrs. Walker turns her back, Daisy's cheeks grow pale, and she seems a "small white prettiness, a blighted grace" (73), too shocked even to be angry. Winterbourne objects to his hostess, "That was very cruel," but he does nothing to counter the ostracism now enforced. He found it "painful to see so much that was pretty and undefended and natural sink so low in human estimation" (78). Winterbourne notes that he is afraid of women such as Mrs. Walker, but not of Daisy. If things were different, he thinks, "if Daisy should love him and he should know it and like it, he would still never be afraid of Daisy...this conviction was not altogether flattering to her; it represented that she was nothing every way if not light." Winterbourne's fear of socially validated power is much more compelling than his half-hearted attachment to Daisy.

A few days after the party Winterbourne encounters Daisy in a garden on the Palatine hill. Spring blossoms and "the freshness of the year" heighten Daisy's charm. Winterbourne ventures to tell the young woman that she will be socially excluded, given "the cold shoulder" (83) if she continues to go about with Giovanelli. The color rises in Daisy's cheeks and she replies, "I shouldn't think you'd let people be so unkind." Her remark reveals the implicit assumption that Winterbourne has a duty to defend her. He declines the task, asking, "How can I help it?"

---

[4]"Grave" appears in the first edition. James substituted "solemn" in the New York edition.

The ambiguities Daisy presents converge a week later in the moonlit Colosseum. Winterbourne enters to find a man and woman seated in shadow beneath the martyrs' cross in the amphitheater. Daisy's voice carries clearly through the night air: "Well, he looks at us as one of the old lions or tigers may have looked at the Christian martyrs!" Her words "settled about him in the darkness like vague white doves" (85). Scriptural associations between the dove and the Holy Spirit suggest that her words contain a truth or insight Winterbourne is unable to clearly apprehend.

When Winterbourne recognizes Daisy, he is "pulled up with final horror now---and, it must be added with final relief." Winterbourne's relief, his sense of "exhilaration for this disburdenment..." sweeps over him. He concludes that Daisy is indeed having an affair with Giovanelli; at that moment Daisy seems "a young lady about the *shades* of whose perversity a foolish puzzled gentleman need no longer trouble his head or his heart." Winterbourne has at last found a satisfactory cliche for Daisy. Her complexities are reduced to "a mere black little blot." As he turns away the young woman calls out: "Why it was Mr. Winterbourne! He saw me and he cuts me dead." Daisy, "lovely in the sinister silver radiance," does not yet understand his reaction. Winterbourne adopts a consciously rough tone to chide the two about the dangers of malaria posed by warm nights in Rome. Daisy, still unaware, declares, "I was never sick and I don't mean to be." As they walk toward the gate, Daisy asks him if he believed, the other day, that she was engaged.

> "It doesn't matter now what I believed the other day!" he replied with infinite point.
> It was a wonder she didn't wince for it.
> "Well, what do you believe now?"
> "I believe it makes very little difference whether you're engaged or not!"

Winterbourne's remark completes the process of putting Daisy outside the circle of significance and signals the collapse of the heroic venture.

When Daisy absorbs the blow she cries, "I don't care whether I have Roman fever or not" (89). As all the foreshadowings of mortality have suggested, Daisy falls ill and dies within a few days. Instead of rescuing Daisy, Winterbourne proves to be one of the "lions and tigers" preying upon the Christians. James's placement of Daisy in the shadow of the cross links her obliquely with the role of heroic victim. The prince would not lay down his life for her, so she must serve as a sacrifice to his cruel gods. Her death is reported in the dialect of her adversaries, "in the laconic, carefully unpoetic language, the social register, of the worldly observer: 'A week after this the poor girl died; it had been a terrible case of the fever'" (Graham 56).

At the funeral Winterbourne learns of his "mistake," his misreading of Daisy. She is buried amid spring flowers in a shady corner of the Protestant cemetery. Her mother relays Daisy's message that she was never engaged, and Giovanelli makes it clear that she was indeed "the most innocent" of women. The revelation "came somehow so much too late that [Winterbourne] could only glare at its having come at all" (92).

The next summer he confesses to his aunt, Mrs. Costello, "It was on his conscience he had done [Daisy] an injury." She would, he realizes, have returned his affection had he offered it. Mrs. Costello says nothing, and Winterbourne concludes: "You were right in that remark you made last summer. I was booked to make a mistake. I've lived too long in foreign parts." Winterbourne returns to his old life in Geneva, and the novel ends with a reiteration of the description of Winterbourne in the first chapter, "A report that he's 'studying' hard—an intimation that he's much interested in a very clever foreign lady."

While most critics persist in balancing the blame, reinforcing the circular equilibrium of the social network, the novel's mythic substructure destabilizes the codes perpetuating the status quo. In this light, Winterbourne's capitulation to social forces appears not merely as muddled ineptitude, but as betrayal. His refusal to play the role of hero throws the moral equilibrium dramatically out of kilter. In saving his "life," his social viability, he has sacrificed his spirit, the beautiful anima figure. His punishment is to be condemned to the wasteland cycle of sterile repetition. Like

Prometheus, Tantalus and Sisyphus, who suffer reiterative penalties, Winterbourne's fate is to continue as the unrealized person he is. The punishment for selfishness is more selfishness.

Whatever the limits of his guilt or banality, Winterbourne's return to the rounds of life in Geneva establishes that Daisy's death has not saved him. At best, he roams in a limbo of lost potential, caught in the empty circle, the zero, of the wasteland. "What shall we do tomorrow?/ What shall we ever do?" Eliot's "Wasteland" creatures ask. Like Hemingway's Jake Barnes and Brett Ashley circling in the taxicab under the perennial sun, like Faulkner's Quentin Compson, crucified on the cycling hands of a clock, Winterbourne spins in a meaningless gyre. Even in the midst of the stoic objectivity of realism, the reader senses the pity of it, the waste of lives endured without myth.

Works Cited

Dupee, F. W. *Henry James.* New York: William Sloane, 1951.

Fogel, Daniel Mark. *Daisy Miller—A Dark Comedy of Manners.* Boston: Twayne Publishers, 1990.

Graham, Kenneth. "*Daisy Miller*: Dynamics of an Enigma," in Pollak, 35-64.

James, Henry. *Daisy Miller.* New York: Charles Scribner's Sons, 1909.

Pollak, Vivian R. *New Essays on Daisy Miller and The Turn of the Screw.* Cambridge: Cambridge UP, 1993.

Seltzer, Mark. *Henry James and the Art of Power.* Ithaca: Cornell UP, 1984.

Weisbuch, Robert. "Winterbourne and the Doom of Manhood in *Daisy Miller*," in Pollak, 65-89.

IF YOU INVITE THE GODS
TO YOUR MARRIAGE

GINETTE PARIS

The imagery of reconciliation is a vast one. As some of you may know if you have had training as a life guard, the most dangerous part in a rescue is when you come close to the swimmer in distress. He or she cannot help grabbing, kicking, clinging to you as if you were a life raft. I've been in that situation twice; it's very scary.

At that moment, even an excellent swimmer can be pulled down and drown as well. That is why most of the training of a life-guard consists in learning techniques to control or literally knock out the other; one learns to give a punch under the chin and to put the swimmer into a judo-type hold that will immobilize him. I now believe that most of the clinging, pulling down, knocking out and immobilizing that takes place between the genders is of that kind.

It's also an image that gives us a different concept of a possible reconciliation than, for example, the metaphor of a war between the sexes. If we use the image of a war, then reconciliation comes in terms of truce, surrender, treaties, a winning and a losing side,

Dr. Ginette Paris teaches in the Mythological Studies Program at the Pacifica Graduate Institute in Santa Barbara, California. This talk was given at "the first Men's Group that extended an invitation to women," The Village of Reconciliation Dancing Ground Conference, Mendocino Woodlands, California, in August, 1994.

both with heavy casualties. We have had this war between the sexes for a long time now; we are still caught in the metaphor each time we present ourselves to the other sex as a victim who demands reparations. But if we imagine that both genders were struggling to get out of deep waters, then we have a different interpretation for what felt, or still feels, so scary. The viciousness of the struggle was bound to happen, because an invisible guilt made us heavy, its sinking weight dragging us down. It is the terrible guilt of a culture that is facing the failure of its basic structure: the family.

We all know that without a space for the young to learn the best things in life—love, generosity, and responsibility—a society is doomed to fail. It is one of the rare points of consensus in all the social sciences that the decadence of the family leads, inevitably, to the decadence of the city, because the city is founded on the family.

Since family has its basis in reproduction and reproduction implies genders, it is no surprise that the most destructive fights between man and woman have appeared under the sign of the family. We tend to forget that we have gone through a revolution. Birth control and the coming into political and financial adulthood of women have made obsolete the kind of rigid gender specialization in the family that some traditionalists are so nostalgic about.

This unavoidable redefinition of society's most crucial unit has been distortingly named the "gender issue" or brought back into a model of gender specialization by calling such communal matters as child care, work sharing, care for the elderly...women's issues.

It is because marriage combines in one space the most intimate bond between a man and a woman and the most demanding social act, an act that underpins the whole society that the temptation to hold the frail human couple responsible for the failures of family is one the community cannot resist.

It seems so logical: the gender connection is the root, the source, the beginning and end of the family structure. So, goes the reasoning, the mess of gender relations must be responsible for the loss of our good solid old family values. "Shame on you, man, and on you woman, who have failed in your gender-specific task.

Look what you've done to the children!" Who wouldn't sink with such a heavy burden of guilt?

Thus the tension between the genders escalates with unceasing loading and unloading of guilt on the other: It's your fault, your feminist anger is too heavy...No, it's your fault, you, the absent father, you weren't there to rescue us...or you, the sexist husband, you wear me down!

Many psychological approaches are no help whatsoever: they persist in relating all problems to the family, while consciousness, that psychological magic arrow, is described in terms of *personal* consciousness, as if the task of becoming conscious were the sole responsibility of individuals.

But what about the unconscious, neurotic, abusive relationship of a community with its families? Let me make a quick disclaimer: by invoking this relationship I am not falling back on that oversimplified attribution, "I'm not responsible! It's Society's fault!" No, what I mean to do is to *change the terms* in which we seek consciousness.

In social psychology, there was once a term to point out the fact that a community or nation, or the whole occidental community, has its own personality; Eric Fromm called it the "social character." Fromm pointed out that this social character serves to channel human energies in certain ways rather than others. A Jungian would call this the collective consciousness.

To my knowledge, aside from our heroic James Hillman who is, as usual, a few steps ahead, few psychologists these days pay much attention to the neuroses of our social character. We are all put to the task of treating our personal guilt over our failures as men, women, parents.

But *something* must be lacking in our social character for us to find no fault with a society that gives a bigger salary to a parking attendant to watch our cars than it pays a kindergarten specialist to look after the next generation.

Collective consciousness is not the simple sum of all our individual efforts to become more conscious. There must be a commitment by the collectivity, a willingness to focus, as we are doing now. There has to be a recognition of our blind spots which asks for the same openness that therapy requires from the individual.

Our society's current pro-family discourse won't do, because it is a defensive denial, as closed to the possibility of making a change as it is to the actuality of change that has already occurred. This discourse is responsible for the constant recycling of guilt and resentment between the sexes.

Let's examine, for a change, a number of blind spots in the collective consciousness that leads to such a disconnected discourse.

One is the community's failure to remember that marriage is not a private act. It is, of course, a place for intimacy, and one can even say that as long as a union produces no offspring, it could remain as private as an affair. But as long as marriage is defined as a contract between the genders for the production or care of the next generation, marriage remains a social act.

A trend began after the last world war of celebrating marriages with a minimum of ceremony, no social fuss, the shortest possible list of guests. This should have been a clue that an aberration was about to happen. Little by little marriage lost its social meaning and became a private act, jealously protected as such.

At the same time, sexuality, especially the sexual affairs of the rich, powerful, and famous, were telescoped by the media, brought out into the public eye and treated as everyone's business. The media love to make a big fuss over a president's possible infidelities, but we are extremely reticent when it comes to discussing the responsibility of the community to intervene in the contract between the genders. Marriage licenses (as a contract between couple and society) have lost all meaning. Even the rituals are gone.

It is a strange development, because at the same time as marriage is given over to the private sphere, the means of fertility control (with all their implications for the continuation of the community) are so much greater. Yet the notion of allowing the community to use these means in order to define what is a fair deal between a gender and the community is still unthinkable.

In my community, a teen-age girl with AIDS decided to experience motherhood before she died and so she got pregnant. The social worker tried to convince her to abort, to avoid bringing suffering to the child, but all that was dealt with strictly privately. At no point was the community involved. It happened that the girl hated her social worker and of course she said it was her own fucking business to have or not to have a child and so she had it.

Any kind of community involvement in such cases is immediately interpreted in terms of fascism, racism, sexism, and all the imaginable evils of big-brother-ism. But this sort of knee-jerk reaction ignores the fact that the community always has had, and always will exert a certain power over the family. This power can be discussed and defined openly, or be exerted covertly, manipulatively, through the economy, for example. To ignore the power of the community in this issue is a perfect case of collective denial.

It is as if, in our marriage ceremonies, only one goddess were invited: Aphrodite, my Valentine, who comes with her mischievous boy, Eros. Of course it is not enough.

In Greek and Roman mythology, one can judge the importance of a ritual by the number of divinities that come to play a part in it. War and politics, for example, call on many gods. But no ritual, no event, not even birth or death, invites as many divinities as marriage. Zeus and Hera, Aphrodite and Eros, Hermes and Hestia, Demeter and Dionysos, each plays a part.

Let us add to the list the unavoidable daughters of Ananke: the Moirae, who weave together the threads that make the complex tapestry of a family's fate, and the Erynes, female monsters with a dog's head and fangs, who avenge family crimes. As for Ananke herself, whose name the Romans translated by *necessitas*, Necessity, she plays her part, too. I find it interesting to note that the Greek word *Ananke* also can be translated to mean something that restricts, like a noose or a yoke, something that binds, as people are bound by their marriage vows, something that ties, like family ties or tying the knot as in marriage. It looks as if Family were another name for Necessity. As Macrobius is supposed to have said, "Love is signified by the kiss, necessity by the knot."

All the many divinities help, and they all make trouble. Which brings me to my second example of a lack in social consciousness. A reality that invites so many powerful gods and goddesses cannot be separated from its shadow. It is unwise to romanticize the family, arousing nostalgia and longing for what exists only in sitcoms and commercials for life insurance or family cars. Such oversimplification is an insult not only to our intelligence but also to the many divinities of marriage. We lose a bit of consciousness every time we forget that even a good, loving, "normal" family teaches us not only the best of human values but also the worst, for it is also in the family that we first learn about rage, shame, rivalries, murderous feelings. It is all in the family; the beauty of the gods and their frightening shadows. No powers exist without a dark side, and when they are denied, murderous feelings become murderous behaviors.

The dark side of family used to be taken care of collectively, by many deep-rooted philosophical anti-family traditions that would help us see the shadows lurking under the surface. Feminism can be seen as one of these traditions, offering many now-familiar instances of severe anti-family criticism. But existentialism, Marxism, and the counter-culture were also anti-family. If we go back even further Plato, Paul of Tarsus, Abelard, Fourier...the tradition is rich.

They may all have been unable to replace the family with something better; but these traditions filled an important function: to remind us that we are all wounded from the start. It is part of being born into a family, part of life.

The anti-family tradition was also the intellectual tool our society used to fine-tune our norms and values, forcing us to make the necessary revisions so that the family, the basic unit of community, stayed connected to what was happening in the community at large. By criticizing the family, an adjustment would come.

Which brings me to a third item on my list, a third blind spot in the collective consciousness: the impact of longer lives on gender identification. Our gender thinking and family values have not yet adjusted to the fact that we live twice as long as we used to!

Choices like marriage or celibacy, sexual freedom or monastic chastity were traditionally the affair of an entire lifetime: you got married, had children, raised them and that was it, your life was over. If you were widowed young enough, you could do the cycle twice. Or you did not marry and by thirty it was too late anyway and you remained the eternal old maid or bachelor.

Those who chose chastity and contemplation would enter a religious order of some sort and be expected to die there. And those who chose to become sexually active while remaining single were usually in the category of prostitute, "kept" mistress, or gigolo, and this was also the kind of choice that defined one permanently.

Only in the last two generations has that pattern been broken on a large scale. I doubt that many here among us tonight has followed only one pattern. All these choices are now *periods* of our longer lives. We live what used to be a whole life before or after raising the kids.

Since marriage and family, which used to give us a gender identification that would last a life time, are now phases in one's life, two consequences are quite predictable: first, that gender identification appear irrelevant in many areas and periods of our lives. And second, in those periods where the archetypal roles of homemaker and breadwinner surface again, that they can detach from the biological gender, leaving us with an archetypal issue and not necessarily an issue between man and woman.

Here, the real tough question is not to accept that we are both masculine and feminine. Given the popularity of Jung's theory on animus-anima, that is almost a cliché now. The tough part is to decide which one of these archetypes— and in which person, at what time and for how long, under what kind of conditions—will have the right to speak out and which one will be silenced, knocked out and immobilized until we reach safety. Who will be told: "Shut up and swim!"

In conclusion, let us remember that revolutionary changes, for example the transition from a complex system like monarchy or tribalism to another, such as democracy, always take many generations to be fully established. Historians have observed that it may take a few hundred years before the old ways die out.

Even the sort of change that might seem easy, like the sudden enrichment of a nation with newly prized export materials, will require two or three generations of adjustments. Imagine, then, the impact of all the revolutionary changes that have happened in the last fifty years, affecting gender.

There is absolutely no point in denying either the changes or the power a community has in helping genders to adapt instead of sinking them in guilt.

Reconciliation will be helped by understanding how we were so extremely dangerous to each other, by our very struggle to survive. Only then can we start the collective work of adjusting the needs of families to the revolutionary changes that have happened in the larger community.

BREAKING THE WILL
OF HEAVEN:
THE ABDUCTION/MARRIAGE
OF HADES AND PERSEPHONE

RACHEL POLLACK

The small town of Eleusis stood just outside of Athens, a day's walk for the mystai, the initiates who would start out from Athens in the morning and arrive at night at the Sacred Precinct. Today, the modern industrial suburb of Elefsis surrounds the Precinct, which lies in ruins since 400 CE, when Alaric and his Goths sacked the temples, apparently to please the Christian bishop. Many archaeological and tourist guidebooks describe Eleusis as destroyed, a mass of stones overpowered by the nearby shipyards and factories. As a result, few visitors make the short trip from the capital. This is both unfortunate and a minor blessing—unfortunate for the many people missing an intense connection with the past, and a blessing for those who wish to avoid the chattering crowds filling the Parthenon. For even though the architecture lies shattered, the very size of the precinct, almost a small village in itself, and the wall which separates

Rachel Pollack is the author of 18 books, many interpreting the symbolism of Tarot cards, and most recently *Godmother Night*, a contemporary novel based on Grimm's Fairytales. Her article, "Aphrodite—Transsexual Goddess of Passion," appeared in *Spring 57*.

it from the modern town, endow it with a power all its own. In a way, the ruins increase the resonance of Eleusis, for they evoke a nostalgic sense of something lost—something which has died and will not return.

When my friend Maria Fernandez and I visited the site we encountered only four other people, a tourist couple who did not stay long, and a mother and daughter from England, the daughter a student living in Greece. Unconsciously, they were acting out the archetype of the place itself, the daughter who separates from her mother, and then returns. Though I did not speak with the daughter, I suspect she came in pilgrimage, for she simply sat, and looked, and listened to the Earth. I did speak with her mother, who told me of her fascination with the idea of past lives, that is, of dying and living again.

In the Hellenistic and Roman periods mystery religions and cults spread through the ancient world. Eleusis, however, retained its status as unique, the actual place where the Mother gave Her two great gifts to the world: the cultivation of grain, and the secret rites of the Mysteries themselves. Some ancient writings hint that the Goddess Herself appears at the end of the rite. And in the Hymn (perhaps we should call a poem to a Goddess a "Hyrrh") Demeter waits for Her Daughter in the temple built for Her by the Eleusinians. As for the grain, and the enactments, the Homeric Hymn leaves no doubt that these occurred at Eleusis.

The Eleusinian Mysteries may have evolved from another ritual, one primarily in honor of Demeter, the Thesmophoria. "Thesmoi" means "laws," after "thesmos," what is laid down, and concerns Demeter as lawgiver, not of civil or human laws, but the laws of nature, of life rotting and growing.

Gaia embodies the archaic Earth, from its earliest moments, through the times of the hunter-gatherers. Demeter, Goddess of agriculture, takes over in a sense, spreading a more complex human civilization. Nevertheless, the laws of death, rot, and rebirth continue. Through the intervention of the Daughter, in Her role as Persephone, Queen of the Dead, the human spirit reaches beyond those laws of disintegration and new life. In this way, Demeter gives the laws of nature, seemingly implacable, but also the transformative laws of human culture and spirituality. We will see as well that the myth of the Daughter separated from the Mother by an intruding male describes the change from unisexual to bisexual reproduction, while the reunion of the two tells us that the Body of life remains whole despite the seeming separation into isolated sexes. The Thesmophoria belonged solely to women. Apollo restricted the Delphic oracle to men. At Eleusis, both men and women took part together. At the same time, all the celebrants, men as well as women, became the Goddess, not the Daughter but the primal Mother, who suffers loss and return.

Two sets of Mysteries took place at Eleusis, the Lesser and the Greater. The Lesser Mysteries, celebrated in winter, prepared the initiate for taking part in the Greater the following autumn. The Lesser focused primarily on the *anodos*, or rising up, of Persephone. As with the Thesmophoria and the Greater Mysteries, the Lesser involved sacrificing a pig, a surrogate perhaps for the initiate's own death.

Many modern discussions of the myth of Persephone assume that She goes down into the ground in winter and emerges in the spring. This would be the case in a northern climate. In Greece, however, much of the land lies barren in summer, the time of drought. Thus, the Greater Mysteries take place around the time of the autumnal, not the vernal, equinox, and they end with water being poured into cracks in the Earth, and the celebrants crying out "Hye! Kye!" that is, "Rain! Conceive!" In ancient Greece, grain was stored during the summer in underground silos. The Homeric Hymn's first name for Persephone, "Kore," means "sprout" as well as the more contextual "maiden."

According to information from archaeologist Donald White, it is not clear what time of the year and how long Persephone remains underground. Some sources do indeed suggest winter, which would hint at a connection to solar as well as agricultural events. The times given range from three months (the summer season) to one third of the year to six months. The Greeks divided the year into three parts, with one of the three as Persephone's time as Queen of the Dead. Karl Kerenyi points out that this breaks the strict connection to grain, since no seed remains four months underground. Persephone's third of the year bore the title "Serpent."

The name Eleusis means either "gate" or "place of happy arrival." Gertrude Rachel Levy identified Eleusis as the Gate of Horn, Virgil's gate of true dreams in the *Aeneid*. "Persephone" means "She who shines in the dark." According to Klein's *Comprehensive Etymological Dictionary of the English Language*, "persona" derives from Persephone, in Her role as guide to dead souls (psyches). Though the English word "person," our sense of an individual self, comes out of persona, we tend to think of "persona" as a fake, a mask. In fact, the word meant a mask worn by the players in Roman drama, but not as a way of hiding their identities. Rather, the personae amplified their voices, while giving them the identities of the Gods or heroes they were portraying.

We know the story of Demeter and Persephone primarily from the Homeric Hymn to Demeter. Other myths give us important hints to implications of the central tale, but the Mysteries themselves derive largely from the Homeric version.

At the start of the story, Persephone bears no name other than Kore, that is, "maiden" or "girl." The poem begins with Her as an innocent, gathering flowers with the daughters of Ocean. Other versions describe Kore as accompanied by Artemis and Athena, virgin Goddesses like Kore Herself. A temple to Artemis and Poseidon stood outside the inner Precinct of Demeter (Poseidon may have been Demeter's consort, for the name means "husband of De (Earth)").

While Kore gathers flowers She does not realize that a trap awaits Her. The God Hades, or Death, has decided He will take Her as His bride, and has persuaded His brother, Zeus, to help arrange this "marriage." Zeus in turn gets the help of Gaia, the Earth, who causes a magnificent narcissus to grow as bait to lure the girl away from Her friends, and from Her mother and anyone who might hear Her.

According to the *Cambridge Illustrated Dictionary of Natural History*, the narcissus is a kind of lily, a flower sacred to the Goddess in many lands, partly from its resemblance to the vulva. Barbara Walker, in *The Woman's Encyclopedia of Myths and Secrets*, associates the lily with Lilith and Astarte, and through Astarte, Eostre. She tells us as well that Mary was said to have conceived

Jesus with the help of a lily. From the *Cambridge Dictionary* we learn that lilies have the characteristic of "dying back to the ground each year," and contain "a superior ovary of many seeds," qualities that relate to Persephone and Her sexual initiation in the Land of the Dead.

The narcissus is one of two plants around which the story revolves. The bright narcissus, with its flower exposed to the air, forms a focus for the world above. And yet, its beauty is illusory, or rather a trick, for it leads to the dark underworld. In the underworld Persephone will eat two seeds from a pomegranate, a plant which conceals its abundance in a dark red shell. Because she has eaten there, she cannot leave for good. Thus, both plants belong to death. A plant cannot give life unless it dies. Just as the lily contains a "superior ovary," so the pomegranate is filled with a chemical very similar in structure to the mammalian female sex hormone, estrogen.

The narcissus brings delight to all who behold it, even heaven and the ground and the seas. But when Kore reaches down to pluck it the land opens up and Hades springs forth in His golden chariot. The God seizes Her and drags Her, screaming, down into the Underworld. Kore cries out for Her father, Zeus, to help Her, "But nobody, no one of the immortals, no one of mortal men, heard her voice." Since Zeus has arranged the abduction, we can say that He refuses to hear His daughter, that the whole world refuses to hear the pain and terror of Her rape. Only Hekate, Goddess of the dark Moon, and Helios, the Sun, "hear" Kore (the Athenians considered Hekate a daughter of Demeter, and thus an alter ego of Persephone). Both of them stand apart from the Gods. As the Sun and the dark Moon they form an opposition complete in itself.

Demeter, of course, hears the anguish of Her daughter, discovers Her gone, and though She "shot out, like a bird, over dry land and sea" no one will tell Her anything. For nine days Demeter wanders, wild with grief, torches in both hands. Because of this search, the Mysteries last nine days, with the middle night a torchlit procession. Nine, of course, is not arbitrary. Three times three, it raises up the Goddess power of the Moon. And of course, in a twelve month year, nine is the number of months in a pregnancy. The Mysteries took place in the last third of the lunar month, when the Moon loses itself to darkness (another time of the snake?), just as Demeter (sometimes identified with the full Moon) loses Persephone.

Finally, on the tenth morning, Hekate, holding Her own torch, appears before Demeter, to tell Her that She heard, but did not see, Persephone's abduction (the name of the Goddess appears here for the first time in the poem). Together, they go to Helios, who puts the blame where it belongs, on Zeus, who "gave her to Hades, his own brother, to be called his wife." Helios advises Demeter not to protest, for Hades will make a good husband, "not unworthy as son-in-law among the gods."

Demeter, however, refuses to reconcile Herself, to surrender. Nor does She try, at this point, to oppose Her all-powerful brother. We might think She would blight the world because of Her daughter, but this does not happen. Instead, She withdraws into Her grief, wandering the world disguised as an old woman. And so She comes to Eleusis.

The royal family takes Her in, accepting Her as a nurse. They offer Her wine, but She refuses, drinking instead a barley drink of Her own creation. A similar drink was featured in the Mysteries, and some believed this "kykeon" contained a hallucinogen which enhanced the revelations at the climax of the rite. Karl Kerenyi points to the refusal of wine as a hint that Persephone's husband secretly was Dionysos, the wine God.

Even if the Goddess refuses wine, a lightness enters the story at this point, as a woman comes to cheer the old nurse. Some versions call her Iambe, the king's daughter, others Baubo, the wife of a swineherd who, according to one version, lost his pigs when Hades took them down with Persephone. Whether Iambe or Baubo, she dances and tells lewd jokes. In the procession from Athens, as the mystai came over a bridge, people impersonating Baubo performed lewd dances before them. Some accounts describe them as women, others as men in women's clothes (possibly both, since both women and men in the rite dressed in simple robes signifying their identification with Demeter).

Except for the possible mystical marriage of Persephone and Dionysos, the dance represents the only directly sexual element in the myth. It suggests the power of sexuality, and life, to assert itself in the face of grief, of death. G. R. Levy tells us that the Greeks sometimes equated the *anodos* of Persephone with the rising from the sea of Aphrodite. Pictures of both show women helping the Goddess to rise up out of the depths—in cosmological terms, to separate Herself from the formless source of being, either of the sea or the Underworld. (Nor Hall writes, "Motherhood is a preparation for maidenhood. Pregnancy is a preparation for virginity." We might add, "Death is a preparation for birth.") The name Baubo means "belly," suggesting a connection to pregnancy as well as the ancient magical movements which have come down to us as belly dancing.

As a boon to the family, Demeter decides to make young Demophoon immortal, a God. Each night She lays the child in the fire, which Her power has charged as an agent against death. In a sense, she defies Zeus, both literally and figuratively. Literally, because we know from other myths that Zeus, like the Hebrew God, did not like mortals being raised to godhood. And figuratively, because Zeus has taken away one immortal child, and now Demeter will replace Her with another. The effort is little more than a gesture, almost of despair, for even if it had succeeded it would not have changed the relations between life and death. Demeter has not yet reached the stage where She will dare to do that.

The godmaking in fact fails, for Demophoon's mother spies on the nurse one night. Seeing her son in the fire, she screams and rushes forward to rescue him. Finally, Demeter's anger explodes—not at the Gods, against whom She still feels powerless, but against wretched humanity. The Goddess reveals Herself and denounces human ignorance, which does not allow us to judge the difference between good and evil. ("Knowing ignorance is strength," writes Lao Tzu, the Chinese sage. "Ignoring knowledge is sickness.")

Demeter demands that the Eleusinians build Her a temple above the Well of Beautiful Dances, the same place where the maidens first found Her and took Her in. There She withdraws, and in so doing blights the world, for without the Mother no plants can grow. There are some subtle ironies in Demeter's action. She, too, had to recognize Her own ignorance, for until Hekate and Helios came forward, Demeter knew nothing of the fate of Her daughter, and while Her anger originates in the loss of Kore to death, Demeter responds by bringing death to the whole world.

According to Kerenyi, some versions of the myth describe Demeter Herself going down to the Underworld to bring back Her child to restore life to the world. In Homer She remains concealed in Her temple. Though She acts against humanity, She strikes the Gods as well. She has upset the natural balance of the world, including the ecology of Earth and Heaven. Just as humans depend on plants to live, so the Gods depend on human sacrifices. Mortal bodies act as a bridge between the raw body of nature and the ethereal body of Spirit. In modern terms we might say that the archetypes feed on the movements and activities of humans in our daily lives.

Demeter's anguish and rage did nothing to alter the decree of Zeus. Her stubbornness, however, her simple refusal to give in and accept death, these finally break the will of Heaven. The gods cannot exist without the sacrifices of humanity. Zeus sends Hermes to the Underworld to retrieve Persephone. Death, however, is not so easily defeated. Pretending to obey, Hades gives Persephone a seed from a pomegranate which She eats before returning to the light. Because of this act, because She has eaten the fruit of the Land of the Dead, Persephone cannot remain in the light permanently but must return every year for a time to Her place alongside Hades as Queen of the Underworld.

The pomegranate figures in other stories besides Persephone's. By the abundance of its seeds, its redness, and its natural estrogen it symbolizes rebirth. And yet Persephone must stay with death because She has eaten it, as if She has allowed Herself to be born in death. During the fast day of the Thesmophoria, the women do eat one food—pomegranate seeds—but only those which have not touched the ground.

When Maria Fernandez and I found broken pomegranates at Eleusis, Maria, deliberately taking on the identity of Hades, squeezed one, pushing out the seeds. The cut, and the white seeds oozing out, resembled the mouth of a corpse, filled with worms.

When the bisexual God/dess Agdisthus severs Hir male genitals a pomegranate tree springs up from the blood. (Some versions say an almond; readers of Grimm's Fairytales may detect an echo of the violent story, "The Juniper Tree," in which a beheaded boy becomes a bird in a tree, either a juniper or an almond; the opening of the story describes the events as taking place "two thousand years ago," a formula very unusual in Grimm.) The blood also impregnates the Goddess Nana, who gives birth to Attis.

A similar story links the pomegranate to Dionysos, and back to Persephone. Dionysos suffers a shamanic dismemberment. Some versions say His heart becomes a pomegranate (Kerenyi writes that the story of the pomegranate tree springing from Dionysos's blood occurs only in late, Christian, commentaries on Pagan beliefs), and when Persephone eats the seed she becomes pregnant and bears Iacchos, whose name the Mystai shout in their torchlit procession during the Mysteries. Iacchos is seen also as the Son of Demeter (a sign that Demeter and Persephone are the same). At the end of the Mysteries the shout goes up that the Goddess has given birth to a son, that "Brimo has borne Brimos." Brimo, and its male equivalent, Brimos, means "strong one." Identities have fused here, the Mother and the Daughter (since the cry does not distinguish which Goddess is Brimo), and the Mother and the Son, by the same name for both. We can describe the Mysteries as just such a fusing of selves, Goddess and mortal, mother and child, female and male, life and death. At the same time, the eating of the seeds of death leads to individuality, for Persephone never quite returns to her unknowing state as the unnamed Daughter of her Mother.

Having become queen in Her own right, Persephone rides Hades' golden chariot back to the light and Her Mother. When She arrives Her Mother demands that Persephone tell the truth, everything that happened to Her. Hearing of the pomegranate seed, Demeter instantly recognizes Her daughter's tie to the Underworld. Nevertheless, She rejoices at Her child's return.

Now She rewards Eleusis, and all humanity. She does not simply restore plant life, but teaches the secrets of agriculture, giving humans control over their food supply. She gives this information to Triptolemos, and instructs him to take the message around the world. Some historians identify Triptolemos with an actual king of Eleusis. The name means either "three times warrior" or "three times plowman," and some see a transformation from one to the other. Kerenyi tells us of Triptolemos's three commandments: Honor your parents, Honor the Gods with fruits, and Spare the animals.

Demeter gives agriculture as a gift to all the world. She gives another gift, just as special, to Eleusis itself—the Mysteries. In the ancient world, anyone might attend the Mysteries, so long as they spoke Greek and had not shed blood. Anyone might take part, but they had to come to Eleusis to do so.

A myth that touches so many levels of our lives—our spiritual yearnings, our sense of ourselves, the very food which keeps us alive—may lead us only to subtle interpretations. Just for a moment, let us look at the story in a different way, as a tale of rape, incest, and resistance.

Judging the meaning of incest in myths becomes difficult when we remember that the Gods and Goddesses in most cultures form a family. Divine energy is One, and only becomes differentiated through the various personalities (personae) of the Gods. Thus, they appear related to each other. When a brother and sister marry or copulate, as the Egyptian Isis and Osiris, or the Japanese Izanami and Izanagi, or Adam and Eve (originally from the same body, they form a "brother" and "sister"), we can see this as the re-union of the split aspects of the divine. However, when a story tells us that a father, or brother, or uncle *rapes* a Goddess, then we can look at the event more in the way we would look at incest in human society.

The significance of rape in the story grows when we find the persistence of rape in the different versions. Demeter, too, is raped. In the Arcadian version of the story, Poseidon rapes His sister, after She has changed to a mare, and He to a stallion. The Goddess becomes Demeter Erinys, Demeter the Wrathful, until, reconciled, She bathes in a river and becomes Demeter Louisa. She bears a daughter, the main figure in the Arcadian myth, but unnamed, called only Despoine, Mistress.

In other versions, Zeus rapes Demeter and fathers Persephone. The God comes to Her as a bull, implying a turnaround (rape as a power inversion) of the Neolithic Cow Goddess and Her Bull consort. Having raped Demeter, His sister, as a bull, Zeus then turns on His daughter/niece, for an Orphic story tells how Zeus comes to Persephone in the form of a snake (Psyche, whose sisters tell her that her husband is really a snake, visits Persephone under command from Aphrodite). Out of this union Persephone bears none other than Dionysos, whom Karl Kerenyi identifies as Persephone's secret lover. In Classical myth Dionysos appears relatively late, but Marija Gimbutas and others have suggested that He actually goes back very far, possibly to the Neolithic. And He appears as both a bull and a snake, the two prime animals of the Goddess from Crete. (To complicate the relations even further, Ovid identifies Demeter's lover, and Persephone's father, as Zagreus, a hunter God from Crete. Zagreus became identified both with Dionysos and Hades.)

Roberto Calasso tells us that Demeter was sometimes considered the same as Rhea—Zeus's mother. In that case, Zeus rapes His own mother, then gives their daughter to His brother Hades. We begin to slide towards the ludicrous here, with Persephone simultaneously Zeus's sister, sister-in-law, daughter and niece. What is important, however, is that Zeus is extending the rule of rape both backwards and forwards in time, to His own mother and His daughter.

Poseidon or Zeus rapes Demeter. Zeus or Hades rapes Persephone. But many mythographers believe Poseidon and Hades were simply other versions of Zeus. The Homeric Hymn implies that Zeus and Hades are the same, for it describes both of them as the "son of Chronos with many names." Thus, Zeus rapes his own sister, and then kidnaps and rapes His daughter/niece. If we think of Demeter for a moment as we would a human woman, we can well imagine Her wild rage and agony. But if we take the Homeric version on face value the pain in the story hardly lessens. For then one of Her brothers, Zeus, rapes Demeter, and another one, Hades, rapes Demeter's daughter. And further, Hades does not act alone. The entire patriarchy rapes Persephone, for Hades first arranges this with Zeus, the Great Father who rules the world. In the story, Hades comes to Zeus and tells of His desire for Persephone. Zeus then sets up the kidnapping. The two male Gods decide who will own Persephone. Again, translate this into a family. The head of the family rapes his sister. When the child becomes a maiden, a younger brother goes to the head and says he wants the child. The two of them then sit down and find a way to arrange this second rape, in secret, so that neither of them will get caught.

The method they use involves the help of Gaia. The Earth causes the glorious narcissus to spring up, luring the Kore into the place where Hades will ride forth from the ground. This may seem strange to us until we remember the ways mothers and grandmothers have betrayed their daughters over and over again in the name of tradition. Some years ago, I read an interview with an Egyptian feminist who described the horror when she was a child and the women came to her with no warning (and certainly no consent), and surgically excised her clitoris. (This practice, so often called "female circumcision," is a misnomer, it seems to me, since the clitoris can hardly be equated with the foreskin.) The woman described how she called out for her mother to save her, only to look up and discover her mother on the side of the knife. This is an extreme example, as are the situations of women sold into forced marriages, prostitution, or slavery. In our "modern" society as well, women reenact Gaia's betrayal whenever they push their daughters to take on roles for which the daughters feel nothing, or to stay with a husband who abuses them, or to keep silent about incest or marital rape, or in the case of lesbians, to suppress their natural desires in order to act "normal."

But if Gaia betrays the maiden, Demeter does not. She rushes through the world, searching for news of her Daughter. In an article on the Mysteries, Pam Wright points out that Hekate alone refuses to take part in the conspiracy. Hekate, the dark aspect of the Goddess, dares both the threat of Zeus, and the terrible rage and grief of Demeter. She alone will tell the Mother what has happened to Her Daughter. Only when Hekate has "broken the silence" (to use a current expression) can Demeter go to Helios and learn the details.

Wright, an educator on issues of child abuse and neglect, points out the significance of truth in the story. When Persephone returns, Demeter tells her, before anything else, to speak the truth, to tell everything that has happened to her. Demeter's absolute commitment to Her Daughter, and to the truth told openly, gives her the power to overturn the decrees of Zeus, enacted in secret. Like women in patriarchal societies, Demeter is powerless to wage war against Olympus. In the end, however, Her will, Her simple refusal to abandon Her child, proves stronger than Zeus's thunderbolts.

The body of the Goddess cannot be destroyed. Paul Friedrich charts the many instances in which the rape of a Goddess produces a daughter, as if when the patriarchal God seeks to break the Goddess, She instead transfers Her power to the next generation. Zeus rapes Leto, who gives birth to Artemis (to Apollo as well, but to Artemis first). Zeus rapes Demeter, who bears Persephone. Poseidon rapes Demeter Erinys, who gives birth to "the Mistress." Another version has Poseidon raping the Gorgon, Medousa, who gives birth to Persephone.

When Hades rapes Persephone, however, something different happens. No child is born (the name "Iacchos" is called out during the Mysteries as the Goddess's child; but the myth describes no birth in the Underworld). It makes sense that no new life should appear in the Land of the Dead. But we also can say that the transference has stopped. Persephone does not surrender Her power and give it over to a daughter. Instead, She finds Her own strength and becomes ruler in Her own right, for while Hades simply presides over the dead souls, He gives them nothing. Persephone gives them comfort, and something more, for participation in the Mysteries promised joy and salvation.

When Zeus rapes Demeter, the Goddess finds Herself powerless. Instead, She takes comfort in Her daughter. But when Hades (Zeus) comes back for Kore, then at last Demeter resists. Thus, by not accepting this further rape, both the Mother and the daughter find their power. And the rest of the world benefits. While Persephone brings us life after death, Demeter brings us life in the form of knowledge, and a deeper involvement in the rain that feeds our bodies.

So far, we have looked at Persephone's encounters solely as terror and destruction, and Her return as a triumph over violence. In a way, this approach assumes Demeter's point of view, as do the Mysteries. But the God who abducts Persephone is Death Himself, and She does not simply escape Him. She becomes intimate with Death, Death's lover, literally taking Death into Her immortal Body. In a way, Death abducts all of us, for no one really expects to die, despite our conscious awareness that we can never escape it. And because of this stubborn belief in our own immunity, Death violates each of us, entering our bodies one by one.

But Persephone does not simply fall to Death. Nor does She defeat Him, in the manner of the patriarchal hero killing the dragon. Instead, She joins with Death, and in so doing becomes Queen of the Underworld. Her way of comfort and promise of new life displace Hades, though officially She rules alongside Him.

We might argue that the Greek idea of the afterlife became dismal and pessimistic as the Olympian religion separated itself from the self-renewing cycles of nature. The Mysteries were able to overcome the terror of death because they restored the identification of human beings with the seed that falls from the dying plant to lie underground, hidden from life, only to spring up, miraculously alive, like the ear of grain shown solemnly to the celebrants at the culmination of the ritual.

The story usually describes Persephone's eating of the pomegranate seed as a mistake, even a tragedy, because it gives Death power over Her. We might better think of it as Her willingness to embrace the reality of Death, as *Her* decision to make Death Her lover.

If we think of Kore/Persephone as a character in a story, and not just a manipulated symbol, then a certain question pushes itself at us. How does Persephone come into Her power? We know what gives Demeter Her power. We know that Her rage, and her love for Her daughter transform Her from a grieving victim to Brimo, the strong one. But what gives Persephone *Her* power? What transforms Her from a nameless "girl" to the Queen of the Dead?

Calasso tells us that "Kore" means "pupil of the eye" as well as "girl," and he suggests that Kore becomes conscious when She sees Herself reflected in the eye of Hades. Let us think for a moment about sight, and consciousness. Narcissus dies when his own image in water captivates him. Kore separates from Her friends when the sight of the flower, narcissus, lures Her away. Thus sight moves both characters away from consciousness and into death.

And then it changes. In death, Kore becomes conscious because She does *not* turn away. Death and seeing are enemies. When someone dies, we close the eyelids. But Persephone looks. Awareness is not something that just happens to us. It is a decision we must make. Kore comes into Her power, She becomes Persephone, the one who shines in the dark, when She chooses awareness in the land of the dead. Death takes Her, as it takes all mortals, but unlike mortals the Goddess does not allow it to obliterate Her. Through Her move into self-awareness She changes the terms of death for all of us—but only if we, too, will become conscious.

Sophocles wrote, "Thrice blessed are those mortals who have seen these rites and thus enter into Hades; for them alone there is life, for the others all is misery" (fragment quoted in Burkert, *Greek Religion*). Those who did not pass through the Mysteries continued to experience death in the old way, as empty shadows. The initiated perceived death in a wholly different way, and so they were saved. Not in the manner of Christ, who saves us all, as long as we give Him permission by "accepting" Him. Persephone asked something more of Her worshippers, that they become fully aware of Her through the nine days of Her Mysteries.

In our time, with the Greater Mysteries long gone from the world, Persephone can become an image of our own awareness. We might think especially of rape and incest. Persephone is the Goddess of those who have suffered violations. The message she gives them is simple: do not become unconscious, do not become mindless. Enter into this death and you will transform it. You will make of yourself something greater than the destruction of your innocence.

Persephone returns through the loyalty and anger of Her mother. But She does not simply return for good, putting Her experience behind Her. Here, too, She comes into Her power, Her name. For how can She shine in the dark if She turns only to the light? She goes down to Hades for part of every year—the time of the Serpent.

I do not wish to suggest that we take so subtle a view of this story that we end up justifying rape. Some modern writers seem to imply that Persephone needs Hades to rape Her so that She might separate from Her mother and become Her own person. In looking for a way out of this problem, Karl Kerenyi's idea becomes significant, that Persephone does not actually join with the shadowy figure of Hades, but the much more vital being of Dionysos. For Dionysos is the God of ecstasy, and to be ravished by ecstasy is very different from being raped by violence. The word "ecstasy" means "to stand beside," that is, outside ourselves, lifted out of the narrow box of ordinary perception. But if ecstasy takes us out of our selves it takes us into our bodies, to the revelations that come when we abandon our selves to the body's desire.

The Homeric Hymn tells us that the Earth gapes open on the Nysan Plain, "named after the Dionysian mountain of Nysa" (Kerenyi). The poem also says that Hades drives Kore across the world in His chariot, before taking Her back down into the Underworld by the river Kephisos, near Eleusis. The name for the place where this happens is Erineos, the word for a wild fig tree which stood alongside. The wild fig tree was sacred to Dionysos, Kerenyi tells us. A mask of the God was cut from its wood in Naxos. (Some people say that the Buddha sat under a fig tree to become enlightened, and that Adam and Eve ate figs, rather than an apple.) Wild fig trees often signified an entrance to the Underworld. Some modern Greeks fear sleeping under a fig tree may bring bad luck, even death.

The philosopher Herakleitos wrote, "Hades is the same as Dionysos." Kerenyi argues that Demeter's refusal to drink wine comes from Her anger at the Wine God who has taken Her Daughter. Most significant of all, an archaic vase painting shows Persephone with Dionysos in a pose which suggests marriage (Dionysos holds out a cup to Her), while Demeter and Hermes look on from the side.

We have seen how the Arcadian version of the myth describes Dionysos as Persephone's *son*. If the Goddess marries Her son, then we are looking at a restoration of the Goddess and Her son-consort. Demeter's consort in Crete, Zagreus, also was identified with Dionysos. Thus, Demeter and Persephone become one, while Zagreus/Hades/Dionysos becomes the lover who dies, goes into the ground, and replaces himself. Once again, we might recall Dionysos's dismemberment. The cutting down of the consort identified the God with the harvested wheat, and the return of the seed to the Earth. In many myths the primordial Goddess becomes dismembered to create the world. We might also identify "Brimos," the Goddess's son, as Dionysos reborn, with Persephone as Brimo, His mother, so that at the end of the Mysteries the circle closes, unbroken. While we do not know the final revelations of the Mysteries, we do know that they involved miraculously grown wheat or barley.

Politically, the myth of Demeter and Persephone embodies the invasion of patriarchal tribes into the old matrifocal order. Where the sacred world previously moved between the Mother and Her Daughter and Son, now the ruling male, Zeus/Poseidon/Hades, seizes control. Demeter resists this change, saying that if Her daughter must die, so will the world. When Persephone returns, She does not restore the status quo; the matrifocal world has vanished. Instead, She brings a triumph over the simple violence of the invaders. Life—the life of the seed willing to return to the ground—becomes stronger than death. Violence cannot destroy the body of the Goddess, for the body is the world itself. Humans who understand the power of life, and embrace it as its twin, death, overcome their fear, and their own terror and rage. They become "thrice blessed," free of fear, free of anger, free to join with the Earth.

Demeter recognizes that She cannot restore the old ways. Instead, She gives Her two great gifts, the Mysteries and agriculture, which together establish human culture on a new level. Kore and Her companions picking wildflowers embody the old way of the hunter gatherers. Demeter's consort in Crete, Zagreus, was called a hunter as well as lord of the Underworld. The circle does not actually close, but opens into a spiral. Demeter goes beyond resistance, to creation. At the beginning of the story, Hades roars forth in His chariot to steal Kore. Persephone then rides back in the chariot without Him. Vase paintings showed Triptolemos riding in his chariot around the world to teach agriculture to humanity. When the "three times warrior" changes to the "three times plowman" the eternal truth of the Mother has transformed the aggression of the original male invaders. According to Anne Baring and Jules Cashford, the vases with Triptolemos sometimes depicted Dionysos on the other side.

We might describe the myth, and the Mysteries, as a way to overcome the guilt of violating the Earth through agriculture. For the plow, as well as the sword, forms an aggression, now directly against the Mother's body. Indigenous Americans and others rejected agriculture because they considered plowing a sin, a cutting open of their Mother's breast. Because Persephone confronts death, Demeter is able to give agriculture as a gift, removing all guilt from humanity.

In a narrow cultural sense, the tale tells of the Indo-European tribes with their warrior Gods overthrowing the thousands of years of Goddess rule in Old Europe. However, the myth also recounts the much wider story of the development of sexuality. For most of the history of life on Earth, reproduction occurred through cell splitting. The "mother" separated into two "daughters," who formed exact copies of the original. At a certain point, a mutation occurred, bringing something new into existence, the male. The male intruded into the perfect unity of mother and daughter.

The development of sexuality brings death. One-celled organisms never actually die, they split, with the daughter a direct continuation of the life of the mother. When both daughters and sons result from combining a male and female parent, they become something new, a unique child that is not the same as either parent, and is more than a combination of the two. But now, the parent dies instead of reproducing copies of itself. Persephone's abduction symbolizes this loss of cellular immortality. Her return signifies the possibility of reconciliation, though not the restoration of the previous condition, for She does not return to Her previous innocence. She has eaten the seed of death, of knowledge. She has become something more than she was, with an awareness, and existence, in the world of the living and the world of the dead.

"The myth of mother and daughter," writes the poet Diane di Prima, "is not a myth of overthrowing (as in myths of the son and the father)...but one of loss and recovery." As such, it speaks to all of us, men as well as women, for we all have lost the unity we knew as fetuses, when we lived within the universe of our mothers' bellies.

At Eleusis, all the celebrants became identified with Demeter. Men who took part were given names with feminine endings. All the mystai wore the same clothes, simple robes which later became used as swaddling clothes for babies. A Roman emperor who had been initiated at Eleusis bore the title "Goddess" on coins showing his face. In the early stages of the Mysteries, the initiates all sat on stools, mourning the loss of Kore, just as Demeter had sat by the well at Eleusis. Becoming Demeter allows all people to suffer the loss of the child, and the joy of Her return.

It is common in our society for women to act out the male myth of overthrowing the father, particularly in the workplace, or other areas where women confront tasks and problems in the outer world. It is less common for men (and even, to some extent, women) to act out the myth of loss and recovery inherent in the Mysteries. For men and women both, the identification with Demeter would have allowed them to experience the pain of whatever they themselves had lost. Women need this as much as men, for the "femaleness" of a myth does not mean that all women automatically experience it. Rather, we all need ways to take the myths into our lives. The fact that as many as several thousand people celebrated the Mysteries, living as a community for nine days, all doing the same things, must have given the final moments an overwhelming intensity.

All people became the Mother in the Mysteries. They also may have identified powerfully with Persephone as She returns at the end, especially if She appeared to them in a vision. And they may have seen themselves in the Son proclaimed at the end, the Brimos who is born to Brimo.

The miracle of reproduction can be described as the one becoming two becoming many. The one-celled organism splits and becomes two, but remains one, for they are the same. With the introduction of the male, a different kind of two becomes possible.

From their union, the many emerge, all the diversity of life. And yet, we carry within us a sense of something lost. Death returns us to the one, for our bodies decay back into the body of the Earth. The collective ritual of the Mysteries gave the celebrants— the many—the possibility to return through a truth other than death.

Bibliography

Baring, Anne and Cashford, Jules. *The Myth of the Goddess*. London: Viking, 1991.

Boer, Charles (tr.). *The Homeric Hymns*. Woodstock, Connecticut: Spring, 1970; 1979.

Burkert, Walter. *Greek Religion*. tr. John Raffar. Cambridge: Harvard UP, 1985.

Calasso, Roberto. *The Marriage of Cadmus and Harmony*. tr. Tim Parks. New York: Knopf, 1993.

Friedrich, Paul. *The Meaning of Aphrodite*. Chicago: Univ. of Chicago Press, 1978.

Gimbutas, Marija. *The Goddesses and Gods of Old Europe*. London: Thames and Hudson, 1974; 1982.

Hall, Nor. *The Moon and the Virgin*. New York: Harper & Row, 1980.

Hall, Nor. *Those Women*. Dallas: Spring, 1988.

Kerenyi, Carl *Eleusis: Archetypal Image of Mother and Daughter*. Princeton: Bollingen Books, 1967.

Lao Tsu. *Tao Te Ching*. tr. Gia-Fu Feng and Jane English. New York: Vintage, 1972.

Levy, Gertrude Rachel. *The Gate of Horn*. London: Faber and Faber, 1946.

Walker, Barbara. *Woman's Encyclopedia of Myths and Secrets*. San Francisco: Harper & Row, 1988.

Wright, Pam. untitled article published in *Fireheart*. (n.d.).

MARRY THE GARDENER!

C. L. SEBRELL

As for that garden where Priapos is to be found (he is the God of gardeners): come on, don't be conned or cozened. The garden is one of the oldest euphemisms for the genital region of women (*pudenda muliebra*), *kepos* in Greek, as we use the word "bush" and images of fruits and flowers, such as fig, melon, apricot, peach, cherry, plum, and of course, rose. So, of course, Priapos is the gardener who cares for the "garden"—a task that keeps him happily occupied.

(Hillman, 43)

Priapus, the ithyphallic god who had statues in his honor in Greek gardens, both public and private, is not often discussed in the context of marriage. Not a deity *of the earth* like Gaia or Demeter, Priapus is a god *of relating to the earth*, taking pleasure in what is natural, earthy, bawdy and lusty. His obvious sexuality has earned him a rightful place in the margins, rather than in the central family of mythology. Priapus isn't to be "domesticated" (Hillman, 46). That's Hestia's domain. His garden remains outside of the house. His is the place that begins at the doorstep and extends through the world. Priapus is outside.

Always just near Hestia, Priapus is a down-to-earth god. The two are a syzygy (although James Hillman seems to think that it

C. L. Sebrell is a doctoral student in Mythological Studies at the Pacifica Graduate Institute in Santa Barbara, California. She is cuurently writing a book on ecopsychology from a priapean perspective.

may be Hermes who is Hestia's counterpart). Hestia, always decent and asexual, is the antithesis of Priapus with a giant erection. The most famous myth of Priapus is that in which he attempts to deflower Hestia. She is sleeping on a grassy knoll, naively exposed and uncharacteristically outside the house. She has entered the garden and is reveling, sleeping in the pleasure of the outside. Just as Priapus is about to mount Hestia, an ass brays and she awakens. The story is a funny one, and she gets away with her virginity intact. Priapus is the only god, of a group of gods easily given over to sex and rape, who is willing to attempt the seduction of Hestia.

Many aspects of Priapus are found in Pan, with one major difference: body. The hairy smelly goat that is Pan, that is all body, gives substance to the reed-like, echo-only nymphs as he passes his arms around them. Pan's half-human body has an affinity for the bodiless, the not-quite-yet-there sort of female. Priapus, however, will have none of that; he will only have a lover with body. No wispy nymphs would please Priapus. Pan, the nature god, and the nymphs of nature are related or at least relatable to nature. Priapus is not an identification with nature but a liaison with it.

Priapus carries the same symbolic objects Dionysus did, a cup and a spear; however, with Priapus, these symbols take on a particularly sexual nature (Murray, 149). Robert Graves calls Priapus "the Pear-trimmer" (-in the same category, presumably, as a connoisseur of "tomatoes") and a god related to Dionysian "fertility" rituals (Graves, 70).

Other sources tell a different story. On closer look, we see a strange and dark god rather than a simple "fertility" figure. Priapus' phallus is not only large, to the extent of freakishness, but it is also crooked (Lopez-Pedraza, 122). Some say that it is bent toward the back. Indeed, Priapus has Dionysian qualities. Dionysian phallic symbols were at the heart of some rituals where enormous phalloi were carried in procession in honor of Dionysus (Vanggaard, 60). But Priapus' is a different type of phallic worship. His bent phallus suggests he is up to something that a *fertility* god would not be—Priapus, it seems, goes for the non-reproductive erotic zones.

Priapus, then, is not a father-type god, nor one with children (or at least none claimed) like Zeus, or Dionysus or Eros himself, but one for whom sexuality is far more than mere procreation. If, as Raphael Lopez-Pedraza says, Priapus is generalized with fertility, the image vanishes. Hillman explains the fertility "cover:" "Scholarship has had to cover this [sexuality] all up with 'fertility' because Priapus is himself covered in order to be displayed (Hillman, 43)."

Priapus' father is a mystery. Aphrodite was less than faithful to her husband, Hephaestos, and she had multiple lovers. Priapus is said, variously, to be the son of Dionysus, Hermes, Adonis and even Zeus. Lopez-Pedraza, in his book *Hermes and His Children*, offers a polytheistic explanation: all of these gods, he says, are the father of Priapus, since there are Priapic attributes in all of them. This approach, however, can lead to Priapus seeming too unfocussed a god in his own right.

Certainly Priapus shares characteristics with Hermes and both can be considered phallic gods in some respect. The trouble seems to come in with the herms or herma, statues of phallic nature placed on boundaries and used to mark property borders. They often are tall and thick with a head at the top, no arms or legs, and an erect penis jutting out. These herms were used also at the doors of houses to guard the property. As a result, almost the first thing one would see when approaching a house was a phallus (Vanggaard, 59). Of course these statues are clearly related to Hermes in that they invoke borders, the difference between "in" and "out."

Lopez-Pedraza, as a result of the association of Priapus to Hermes and Aphrodite, says that it is possible that Priapus *is* the Hermaphroditus. He gets this idea from Carl Kerenyi's book, *The Gods of the Greeks*. In it Kerenyi says, "Priapos, too, was numbered amongst the sons of Hermes, and it was claimed for him that he was none other than the Hermaphroditos" (176). Kerenyi goes on to claim that this association existed because Priapus was a "creature excessively phallic, and indeed phallic to the rear." Kerenyi relates that a "herdsman had found the monster . . ." yet concludes that the herdsman had recognized "the particular position of his phallic organ—in other words, that characteristic which was not merely phallic, but Hermaphroditic." But the erect male organ is sometimes naturally curved back this way during tumescence. This sometimes famous bend may only show that Priapus is a uniquely endowed erotic god. Yet not a hermaphrodite. Why Kerenyi concludes this is somewhat of a mystery better left to Freudians.

Many of the books that consider the cult of Priapus or any type of phallus worship try to apologize away the sexual, humorous, and illicit nature of Priapus. The cult of Priapus was not a cult of creation, regeneration and procreation, but a cult of love in the sexual sense. It may have been a cult not so much of reckless abandon (like Dionysus) but of a cultivated, even sensitive, virile and skilled lover. He was a lover of the feminine earth, not a god or goddess that controlled or possessed it.

While it is not easy to find Priapus in Greek mythological texts, most information about Priapus is found in the *Priapea*, a collection of poems from Latin origins in which many of the nuances of Priapus' character are put to verse and lewd and lascivious subject matter is couched in correct poetic forms. Many translators "clean up" Priapus' language. It is thus tricky to study Priapus. Yet Priapus may have been a much more important god than is today given credit.

It is all the more interesting that the only people who seem to want to discuss Priapus today are feminists, especially those arguing that Greek and Roman life was patriarchal and misogynist. (See Eva Keuls' book, *The Reign of the Phallus*.) A focus on the phallus is not always the glorification of an anatomical part that women do not have. (The attraction or aversion to a virile, strong phallus is, of course, not limited to females, as gay men, too, are interested.) In antiquity, the cult of Priapus was actually maintained by women (Brown, 87). In fact, few understood the intricacies of Priapic worship better than the "good women of Isnernia" (Stone, 108).

Priapus today may have more to say to those of us who are concerned for the earth itself. After all, the failure of most of us to relate to the planet itself is psychological, not wholly political and our relationship to the earth is based to some extent in our relationship to our bodies. "The divisions issuing from the division of body and soul are first sexual and then ecological" (Wendell Berry, 113). Nature is always viewed as feminine but it is not the female body we are alienated from so much as the body in general, *our* bodies. And Priapus, ecology's mythical gardener, is certainly a god who leads us away from a bodiless ecology. The planet is not only in our hands but it is in his hands, too. Instead of an infantile "return to the Mother," with Priapus we get a gardener. (Now maybe something will get done!)

Look at the bodiless' garden's strange history. Renaissance exploration and colonialism put an end to the idea that the Garden of Eden was somewhere (literally, geographically) on earth. It had always been understood that the Garden was on this planet. Myths that told of an Earthly Paradise existed long before the Bible was written, but the Book of Genesis tells of a geographical place for the original Garden of Eden (Delmeau, 10). For centuries people searched for the historical place. When technology made the earth seem more manageable, theologians of the Renaissance began to discuss a paradise that was in the heavens.

But a physical paradise had its risks. Earthly gardens were too sexual in nature: The imagery associated with the garden was loaded with nudity, physical pleasures and license, forbidden fruit. Slowly, the sensuality of the heaven in the garden was weeded out. Monks who described a paradise based on a hierarchy of pleasure were followed by monks who denied the existence of "celestial flesh" (McDannell, 136-7).

Just as the garden was being launched into the starry heavens, Vesalius was inventing modern anatomy. The dead body became a corpse (Romanyshyn, 17) while the mechanical functional system applied to the body turned the heart into a pump, the central nervous system into an electrical unit, the brain into a command center and muscular structure into a robot fired by pulses of electricity. Like the Garden of Eden on earth, anatomical exploration found no soul within the body. Like the Garden on earth, the soul couldn't be located, mapped, touched or dissected.

Imagining the body as a separate entity from the soul rendered the body nothing but a shell, a temporary resting place that could be abused, neglected, polluted. "As a thing, the body is denied any dimension or rightful prescience or claim in the mind. The concerns of the body—all that is comprehended in the term *na-ture*—are thus degraded, denied any respected place among the 'higher things' and even among the more exigent practicalities" (Wendell Berry, 113). The language used to describe the soulless state of the body resembles the language used to describe the Gar-denless state of the earth. Ecology needs its gardener back.

"Healing is not possible...unless we can maintain conscious, bodily connection to the Earth, so we must start with the recog-nition that this connection is severed; here is where healing must begin" (Sardello, 128). But in even more obvious a sense—as every exercise article will tell you—gardening is good for the body. A garden on Earth, for anyone who sees things mythologically, means a physical connection with the divine. So what happens when you start cultivating your "gardener?"

There is a lot of discussion today about unwed mothers and the price Americans pay to support them. It is said that twenty five per cent of births in this country are to single mothers. Seventy five per cent of births are, then, to married couples. Priapus, the gardener extraordinaire, gives women (and men) another image to think about. But what about couples who make the decision not to have children? This decision often means a "new" type of sexu-ality, one not entrenched in reproduction. Is Priapus the god of this type of marriage?

Priapic love is different from traditional sexuality in several ways. Priapic love is not an "ensnaring" experience. Stereotypical Dionysian sex is an entrapment: his victims cannot seem to help themselves. The daughters of Minyas, possessed by Dionysus, were ensnared by grapevines and drank wine that was dripping from the ceiling. These self-controlled and upright ladies were suddenly transformed into wild, raving lunatics driven mad by a Dionysian sensuality. Priapic love is not quite so toxic.

Priapic sex has such an honesty, because it has unashamedness about the body, that it often evokes a sense of humor. In such light, (not Aphrodite's misty, pink light) sex is funny. Priapic love is a comical pleasure, disrobed of pretense. The Aphroditic pressures we put on love encounters to be romantic, cosmic, earth-shaking, something "much, much more than ever dreamed of," are gone from Priapic love. But gone, too, are the Romantic illusions that make many marriages fail.

Priapic love balks at the Platonic idea that we are all in search of a soul mate, the one that will make us complete and whole. Priapeans, to be shamelessly blunt, are in search of a phallus! (This is a "big" (!) topic for such a small paper, so I won't go into how we might deliteralize the phallus just as we have learned to deliteralize the soul.)

With Priapic love, there are no unplanned pregnancies, no groping in the dark, no need for that always elusive "spontaneity" that balks at contraceptives. Intoxication and unprotected sex are not for Priapus, either, who only wants pleasure in the art and skill of lovemaking and a little more "care" for his long-neglected garden.

Love is often called a "transmutative process that we are each called to by the purifying fire of Eros, of longing for peace and wholeness" (Versluis, 71). But Priapic love doesn't purify, it satisfies. Since Priapic love demands that you be whole and complete *before* you come together, chances are your marriage won't get burned in Eros' fire any more than the planet itself will.

Works Cited

Berry, Wendell. *The Unsettling of America: Culture & Agriculture.* "The Body and the Earth." San Francisco: Sierra Club Books, 1977.

Brown, Sanger. *Sex Worship and Symbolism of Primitive Races.* Boston: Badger, 1916.

Delmeau, Jean. *The History of Paradise.* New York: Continuum, 1995.

Graves, Robert. *The Greek Myths I and II.* New York:Penguin, 1960.

Hillman, James. "Pink Madness." *Archetypal Sex.* Spring 57. Woodstock, Connecticut: Spring Publications, 1995.

Kerenyi, Carl. *The Gods of the Greeks.* Great Britain: Thames and Hudson, 1979.

Keuls, Eva. *The Reign of the Phallus.* Los Angeles: University of California Press, 1985.

Lopez-Padraza, Rafael. *Hermes and His Children*. Switzerland: Spring, 1977.

_____. *Priapus*. The C.G. Jung Institute of Chicago. Chicago: Audio tape, 1984.

McDannell, Colleen and Bernhard Lang. *Heaven: A History*. New Haven: Yale UP, 1988.

Murray, Alexander. *Manual of Mythology*. New York: Tudor, 1935.

Parker, W. H. tr., ed., *Priapea: Poems for a Phallic God*. London: Croom Helm, 1988.

Romanyshyn, Robert. *Technology as Symptom and Dream*. New York: Routeledge, 1989.

Sardello, Robert. *Love and the Soul*. New York: HarperCollins, 1995.

Stone, Lee Alexander. *The Worship of Priapus. The Power of a Symbol*. Chicago: Pascal Covici, 1925.

Vanggaard, Thorkil. *Phallos: A Symbol and Its History in the Male World*. New York: International UP, 1972.

Versluis, Arthur. "Ficino's Garden." *Parabola*, Winter 1995. Vol X, no. 4.

Zimmerman, J.E. *Dictionary of Classical Mythology*. New York, Bantam, 1971.

from WHAT CAN WE ASK OF MARRIAGE?

HELEN G. HENLEY

M arriage is the foundation stone upon which rests almost every culture of every tribe or nation that treads this earth. Its forms vary immeasurably, but its essential social purpose is always the same: namely, to foster the institution of the family and through the family to ensure that the needs of the community shall be sustained from one generation to the next. It is surely not to promote the happiness of the wedded pair that marriage is supported by a governing body. Its legal purpose has nothing whatever to do with human relationships. The basis of marriage is social, and this had been true since time immemorial, when the dark of dawn of a prehistoric world found human marriage already in existence. Even then it may well have been early man's inheritance from some ape-like progenitor, and our own primordial ancestors may never have devised marriage at all,

Helen G. Henley was a leading figure in the Analytical Psychology Club of New York, to which she read this paper on March 18, 1949. It was published in the 1950 issue of *Spring*, which was founded by the Club in 1941 and has been in continuous publication ever since, making it the oldest Jungian journal in the world. We are proud of *Spring's* long tradition of publishing thoughtful papers in archetypal and Jungian psychology and from time to time we like to reprint relevant excerpts from the best of these as part of a series called *50 Years Ago in Spring*.

but have accepted it as a natural condition of life. As to that no man can say. We can safely conjecture, however, that the human pair of great antiquity made their first commitment to responsibility for others of their own kind through some simple, crude structure of family life. The anthropologist, Westermarck, tells us in his *History of Human Marriage* that "...marriage and the family are intimately connected with one another; it is originally for the benefit of the young that male and female continue to live together... We may truly say that marriage is rooted in the family rather than the family in marriage."[1]

"For the benefit of the young." Has not this necessity provided the basis for marriage throughout all the ages? From remotest antiquity the young could derive from the communal life of the family in essence what it offers them today. In the beginning, as now, there was food and shelter, perhaps animal skins for their bodies, guidance in those pursuits wherein they would presently need to become proficient. They must have been allowed to play, too, like cubs of the lesser animals. And in one regard they had doubtless advanced quite beyond other creatures: in the instinct to worship, which is born in the simplest human soul. The life giving sun as I rose each day in the heavens must have stirred the earliest archetype of God. These were the centered interests of collective man early in human history. And despite all that mankind has learned and experienced and devised since its beginnings, this is where the centered interest of collective society reposes still. Food and clothing, shelter, play, social responsibilities, guidance in the communal way of life - a connection with one's church; do not these general categories cover the interests of most of the human race, as they did in remote antiquity when the first marriage was "rooted in the family" only because there were children? Collective man knows nothing of psychological relationship in marriage. By virtue of his very collectivity he could never grasp the mature meaning of relationship. To him the good marriage must be historical in character, tending to continue the manner of life of the ancestors. It still seeks to follow archetypal

---

[1] Edward Westermarck. *The History of Human Marriage.* 5th ed. 3 vols. New York: Allerton Book Co., 1922. Vol. 1, 72.

patterns, unreflectively as ever, and preserve old customs unchanged. For the body of mankind, such a way of life is entirely possible, since the form of wedlock is everywhere indigenous to its own soil and held sacred there. Thus it becomes assured that father and mother assume the roles that native tradition has assigned to them. Man's place is never questioned, nor is woman's, as husband and wife join the procession of the ancestors.

There has never been a distinctively American archetypal pattern of marriage; for us no single ancestral form of wedlock springs out of a soil which gave it birth. All Americans, either individually or ancestrally, have emigrated from other land; and in our whole span of life on this continent society has been confronted with the problem, one might also say, of jockeying man and woman into roles dictated by time and place. Was not the pioneer woman of 1620, and for years to follow, often called upon to shoulder a musket? And if one takes a hurdle across the centuries, is not the young father of today frequently caught in the act of diapering the baby? With us, immediate conditions of life have determined what must be a man's responsibility, what woman's. And with the result that American marriage has been in continual process of change....

The status of women in marriage may be said categorically to keynote the general pattern of life within the boundaries where it is observed. In early America the husband was absolute ruler of his household. He was legal owner of the children and the property, and could claim the right to assert his authority over the wife whenever it pleased him to do so. As time went on many of these conditions changed, except in the matter of formal education for women. Until about 1800 only the Quakers would grant to the girls the right to go to school. Previously it had been considered enough for a girl to learn from her own mother whatever the latter could teach of writing and reading and sums. Throughout the 19th century, however, such conditions were palpably altered. And for this, two factors were largely responsible: one economic, the other educational. Between them they brought about the great enantiodrama in the life of American womanhood. But they opened Pandora's box! To speak first of educational changes: When in 1821 Emma Willard founded her "Female Seminary" in Troy, New York, the declaration of intellectual independence for woman was signed and sealed; that shaping of modern American woman was on its way. And with the numinous appearance of Mt. Holyoke and of Vassar colleges, a laurel crown was laid upon her head. They called it a mortarboard. Higher education for women subsequently became the greatest single factor in altering the general relationship between sexes, with consistent changes in the psychology of our marriages. But there was yet another factor destined to exert its boundless influence over life in America. By 1850 power driven machinery was introduced and the money-making era dawned. A "dollar aristocracy" now came into being. Cities grew, and in the homes women were freed from household drudgery to reshape their domestic destinies. Husband and wife now find themselves in new relation to one another, one in which the wife emerged as manifest standard-bearer of her husband's material success. This she proclaimed in her dress, her house-furnishings, the table that sparkled with damask and silver and foreign wines. The exaltation of American wifehood had begun. To the women of good background the best and finest had, of course, never been a novelty; but in the mid-nineteenth century prosperity overspread the land in Sears and Roebuck proportions and gave new importance to the woman. But how outwardly oriented became the pattern of marriage! We have only to look at the wedded pair in *Life with Father* to see how the persona fashioned their social code. This marriage is characteristic of its time largely because so little of the inner world of either partner seemed to have a place in it. And the inner world is nature. Without it the opposites in the psyche are quite thrust apart; conventions on one side, the instincts on the other. In the Victorian era when artificial attitudes made for pattern morality - when for example, such plays as *East Lynn* expresses the accepted code - many a marriage found itself in such a state of cleavage. Under the rigid laws of totem and taboo the instincts were too often repressed beneath the lock and key of shame and make-believe and fear. Yet down in the dim "red-light" districts of cities could be found an outlet that made mockery of lock and key, where man sometimes went for coarse fulfillment of their sexual urge, their wives being merely "ladies," who excluded human instinctiveness and reserved a sex life for the end of childbearing alone. What unconscious deception and self-delusion lay behind these attitudes! One of the gravest evils of this false tissue lies here: that it drives a wedge between man and wife often enticing and diverting unconscious energy toward the children. When the mother's unconscious interest becomes centered in her son the reenactment of the Cybele-Attis myth draws dangerously near. Then the wife is transfixed at a biological level, maternal rather than womanly, her libido diverted into dark unconscious channels. Sometimes when she holds her child so close - often it is the son - that his very nearness seems to fulfill her. Again she is the mother to her husband, enfolding him with arms that cradle his immaturity. This is the theme song of many a psychic drama on the American scene, born, it seems to me, of the fact that our 19th century women were showered with much of the world's goods and with little responsibility for what held substance. The 19th century was a fabulously unreal period in our history and we have had to answer for it. Our subsequent marriages have too often collapsed for lack of inner cohesion. But we Americans are not slow actually to deal with problems; only slow to recognize that we have them.

A conscious relationship must always presuppose two individuals able to make a commitment to a meaningful life together. Each has his own contribution to make that life. But growing relationship does not follow a smooth and even course; because a man or woman, who is sincerely self-acceptant, must often express the dark aspect of his nature without which he can never become himself. For nobody is whole without negative qualities and one begins to grow free only through the assimilation of the shadow. In that process of assimilation other persons in one's environment are the immediate "beneficiaries!" And the husband or the wife is the first in line. Conscious relationship is always dearly won. It's achievement is both an art and a discipline, seldom consummated in the early years of married life. First - so goes the rule - bride and groom find themselves in an enchanted garden of young love. But between blossom time and harvest lies summer with its blistering heat and its wind and storm, the trial season which must be weathered if the harvest is to bring forth ripened fruit. In the marriage also there must be a testing time when crucial matters arise to challenge the very fundamentals of relationship. When such hazards can be overcome with mature consciousness, then the adult relationship ripens.

In an unpublished lecture, Jung makes the observation that, "Individuation always means relationship." Consciousness, or individuation, is sought through the attempt to realize one's totality, in an effort to attain the Self. And since the very nature of individual consciousness rests upon the union of opposites, the Self must be essentially related both to consciousness and the unconscious. The mature personality therefore is in touch not only with his inner world, but also with the outer. O speak of this fact superficially here since it could too easily be assumed that to be conscious in marriage is to be out of touch with "Our Town." Nothing could be farther from the truth. WE should be in a bad way indeed if we lost our place in the world of men to be cloistered instead in a hot-house of seclusion. The point is that we must relate, and not identify, either way.

And now, in conclusion, I turn again to the status between the sexes; this time as it stands today. You will recall that early New England marriages found the husband in an altogether dominant role - the situation which first characterized the relation between man and woman in America. By the middle of the 19th century this initial juxtaposition had in a sense reversed itself; and the woman, often by indirection to be sure, found herself in the leading role. And now, as the 20th century reached its midpoint, we find a tendency towards rather more equilibrium between the sexes. Education and a firm place in the economic world, with increasing proficiency in many fields, have provided woman with far more realistic concerns than in the days when intrigue and wire pulling were the major preoccupations of the animus. When he serves the woman, and she is no longer merely doing his bidding, the animus proves himself an individual asset. Then he no longer represents a counterfeit Logos, but helps a woman to realize a truer masculine principle within herself. Conversely, in some men there is a growing realization today of certain life values hitherto obscured by an anima attitude which touched off only the emotions and rejected feeling, as woman's sentimental folly. I certainly do not mean to submit that the principles of the opposite sex are highly developed in either man or woman today. But each is more potentially available than in the days when the sexes viewed one another as psychologically antipathetic. The two world conflagrations doubtless had something to do with this, both during the war years and in their wake. But though one might long to have it otherwise real relationship has not yet become the standard goal in American marriage. Life's uncertainties are too widespread and too deep. When we speak of marriages today we have to differentiate between the older ones and those contracted within the last decade. For the older generation felt security in the future of the world; they could still pool their efforts and ambitions and their worldly goods, tie them together with a little love and go ahead in their adventure of life with high hope. They could trust life, somehow. Today the future looks vague to many young married people and they venture no predictions for it. I believe this fact is connected with the characteristic difficulties which many young persons in wedlock have been experiencing. They are thrown upon the moment and stake too much on what it can offer them. They grow restless, indifferent, sensuous - sometime orgiastic - discontented with life and one another, and unconsciously perhaps, with themselves. To repay their wartime service and sacrifice they can't even find homes to make attractive. One sees their dilemma plainly enough, but that doesn't alter the facts. If we look into the heart of the trouble we may expect to find it rooted in the Eros problem, regardless of outer conditions. Not yet having learned that the only security the human heart can ever know must lie within oneself they break their marriages, one out of three, and carry the Eros difficulties unmodified into the next environment they find for themselves.

In any situation touching human relationship there are certain root considerations to bear in mind. And especially is this so in marriage. When matters of mutual concern arise between the partners there are always Eros observances to remember. Of prime importance is the simple Eros lesson that when problems arise between them both should agree to deal with the situation, generated by such problems, as though it stood before them objectively, thereby obviating the animus and anima duel that threatens every time the partners grow tense and personal. If this one rule could be observed from the beginning I think it would materially cut the divorce rate! Also, under the law of Eros, unless the ego can take second place, negative attitudes are automatically generated. The sense of well-being in marriage cannot survive the demand for an abnormal ego importance on the part of either participant. Eros must have an important place in the sex life of man and wife; for without the mutual consideration and concern which relatedness provides, the partners find themselves in mere biological connection. Then, regardless of the nature of their sex life - whether it be fiery, indifferent or cold - by itself it is without human meaning for the marriage. Love doesn't survive unless it is called upon to vitalize all aspects of human relationship.

And now I want to make a plea for zest, for a bit of enthusiasm to bring to the living of everyday. Jung tells a story to show how torpid life could be without zest. It is of a certain pious man who asked for God to remove the spirit of passion from the world. Now God can never resist a pious man so he removed all passion. Then the man discovered that the roses in his garden were no longer fragrant, that his wine had lost its flavor and the kisses of his young wife were no longer sweet. So this pious man quickly saw his blindness and prayed God to let passion come back again.

Relatedness is never fully achieved until each partner recognizes that "Eros has claims as well as obligations." Genuine give-and-take is the Eros law. Some natures find it easy to give, difficult to receive; and though such an attitude may pass for generosity it isn't that at all, but an expression of inertia. The partner finds it less troublesome to make no demand for himself and so creates an impediment to Eros. No, in a balanced relationship each one needs to make both claims and concessions; to know what belongs to him, what to the other. Primarily each must claim his full measure of privacy, otherwise husband and wife intrude upon one another and the marriage begins to list in the direction of "Our Town." Then it loses its individual meaning, and "it is only the meaningful that sets us free." The marriage that sets each partner free has truly won its laurels. I hope nobody will construe what I am saying to signify that granting freedom is equivalent to being indifferent. On the contrary, to concede the right of freedom may ask a profound sacrifice but leaves man or wife the right to grow whole without benefit of shaping by the partner.

AN INTERVIEW FROM ISRAEL

EREL SHALIT

The editorial board of Wisdom—wherefrom? *(tentative name of the Bulletin of the Israel Association for Analytical Psychology) decided to conduct interviews with prominent members of the society. I decided to jointly interview the two senior, male, Jungian Analysts Yechezkel Kluger (who died in December, 1995) and Gusti Dreyfuss, both former Presidents of the Israel Association for Analytical Psychology, each with a long and productive record of analysis, training, teaching and writing. Their professional histories have touched upon and been intertwined with the (post-war) development of analytical psychology, and they have each had personal meetings with Jung.*

For editorial reasons, I have taken the freedom to make cuts in the interview, while trying to retain the tone and the essence of what I was told.

Initially I wondered what brought each one of them to Jungian psychology and to the Zürich Institute, especially in the wake of World War II. Both are imbued with a strong sense of Jewish awareness, and accusations of antisemitism were levelled at Jung already at the time. I assumed it took courage, a conscious decision, or maybe a synchronistic, meaningful experience to lead one to Zürich.

Erel Shalit is a clinical psychologist and Jungian analyst in Ra'anana, Israel. He is the author of *The Hero and His Shadow—Psychopolitical Aspects of Myth and Reality in Israel* (in Hebrew, 1995), and co-editor of *The Bulletin of the Israel Association for Analytical Psychology,* where this interview, conducted at the home of Yechezkel Kluger on October 25, 1994, was first published, in Hebrew, in January, 1995.

Yechezkel Kluger (YK): It was quite accidental. I became interested because of my own analysis. Why Jungian analysis? Because
of my then 7 year old daughter. I was living in Los Angeles. At a
parents' meeting of her Hebrew school I met the father of a boy.
My daughter is Nomi, this kid was Tom. I talked to the father,
Dr. Kirsch, a Jungian analyst. Later I went to see him. That's how
I got into Jungian psychology. (That kid in Hebrew school was
Tom Kirsch, [former] president of the IAAP). Purely accidental -
if he had been a Freudian, I would likely have become a Freudian.

   After several years in analysis I wanted to become an analyst. At
that time a Psychology Club had been formed in L.A. around Dr.
Kirsch and his wife, and Dr. Zeller, and I was invited to become a
member.

Gusti Dreyfuss (GD): I made my matriculation in 1940. I wanted
to study medicine, but the director of the school said that with
the Nazis only 40 km from Zürich that is no good. Wherever
you go, you can't use it, and the Jews will probably not be able
to stay in Switzerland. He recommended I study at the famous
technical high school, and whatever you learn there is accepted all
over the world. I studied chemical engineering and hated it. Following my mother's (!) advice I did a doctorate in textile engineering, hoping to join my father's factory, where for better or
worse I could be the son of the boss. But it wasn't for me, so I
went to study (after work!) Industrial Psychology, at the Institute
for Applied Psychology, but that also wasn't for me. The Director suggested I go into analysis, and referred me to the well-
known Dr. Liliane Frey, in 1946. Because of the analytical work,
e.g., with dreams, active imagination and after a few years in
analysis, she suggested I register at the Jung Institute. Aniela Jaffé
was the secretary. I started in 1950, and the first course was on
Anima and Animus, with Emma Jung.

Going to Zürich

*Today the Jungian world is well-established, with training programs
in many places, with different strands of Jungian (or post-Jungian)*

orientations. In the early 1950s, however, there was Zürich (and even today Zürich-trained analysts may be surprised that you can train elsewhere).

YK: In 1951 the L.A. Club invited Dr. Rivkah Schaerf, one of the teachers at the Jung Institute (in Zürich). Now we would get something first hand from Zürich. There was a big reception at Max Zeller's house. Earlier, having become a Zionist during my studies at medical school I thought the Jews had too many doctors and needed farmers. My wife and I went to Israel in 1935, and became members of kibbutz Na'an. In 1937 I went for a "short visit," that lasted a long time, to the States. I had quit medicine, so I studied optometry to earn my fare back.

While in analysis we had spoken about my Hebrew name (Yechezkel) and about Zionism. Dr. Kirsch told me, "Your Zionism, your Israel is an internal Zionism, an internal Israel." I felt a conflict. I was given a transcript of a book by Rivkah Schaerf. Besides feeling close to the subject itself, "Satan in the Old Testament," it did something more to me, a feeling of kinship. Here was a Jungian analyst, and her name was Rivkah. At this reception for her, I approached her. Not knowing Swiss formality I said, "Hello, Rivkah, I'm Yechezkel." She looked at me with a shocked look. We had not even been introduced and I addressed her by her first name! "If looks could kill, I would be dead by now," I told my friend.

That's how my relationship with Rivkah started. During her two visits that year we became very friendly, and she encouraged me to come to Zürich to study, in 1952. As foreigners we could study full time, so I could finish in three years, being one of the first five or six graduates from the Institute. I remember asking Jung to sign my diploma. I was working with his wife at the time, and once in a while I was seeing him. He said, "No, I'm not a member of the Curatorium." I said, "Yes you are, you are the Honorary President," and I took out the diploma to write "Honorary President." He said "No no, I'll do it myself," and wrote "Honorary President, C. G. Jung." That's the only diploma with Jung's signature.

GD: I had two personal interviews with Jung. I had been told that Rivkah (Schaerf at the time) gave a course on Job, which my wife and I attended in 1949, i.e., before I registered at the Jung Institute. In fact, I came to know her quite well, and so I didn't prepare myself well enough for an exam on mythology and religion, and I failed!

Jewishness and Analysis

Today the question of Jung and anti-semitism is laid bare on the table. In the wake of World War II it must have taken no less courage and reflection to confront the conflict between being a Jew and simultaneously to train as a Jungian Analyst. Or, may it be that this particular branch of psychology and psychoanalysis may enable an analysand/trainee to bridge the conflict, to connect up more deeply and meaningfully with one's religious heritage, in spite of external contradictions?

GD: In the course of analysis I had several dreams.* The outcome of this inner work, as well as the impact of the stories I had heard from Jewish refugees from Germany and Austria already in 1938, was that I decided to come to Israel. My Jewishness was activated in analysis, though in analysis with a Christian. I met Sigi Hurwitz around 1949-50, going to Eranos. We had a common interest in Jewish material and Jungian psychology. I felt a need for analysis with a man and a Jew, and Liliane Frey suggested I see Erich Neumann (who used to come to Switzerland every summer), which I did in the summer for a few years.

YK: As a matter of fact, though I started analysis with a Jew [James Kirsch], he didn't encourage my Zionist feelings. He was quite knowledgeable in Jewish matters [e.g., James Kirsch: *The Reluctant Prophet*]. He had been in Palestine as a refugee from Germany and worked here for half a year, but apparently it didn't click with him. Then he went to England and later to the

---

* [published in Spiegelman & Jacobson (Eds): *A Modern Jew in Search of a Soul.*]

States. Jungian psychology became his quasi-religious center. Jung was very Christian in his psychology, and I think that had an effect on Kirsch, too.

GD: I felt very close to my maternal grandfather, whom I went to synagogue with as a boy. However, the texts didn't mean anything to me. I wondered, what did the special sacrifice, as in the prayer of Musaf [the "additional service" on the Sabbath], mean? Jungian psychology opened me up to the symbolic attitude, to understand on a psychological level what was going on in the prayers. It was analysis, my friend Sigi Hurwitz, and the lectures of Rivkah, that opened me up to the Jewish symbols.

YK: I also had a traditional Jewish upbringing, e.g., putting on phylacteries, until I went on preparation for living in the kibbutz. Then my Jewish feelings became more nationalistic. However, I didn't have the same problem as Gusti, accepting the prayers the way it was. It doesn't talk to a young person of this century if he doesn't have a real, basic, deep Torah-education, which neither of us had, and I miss it. And it is tragic. Though both Gusti and I write on Jewish themes, we don't know enough, e.g., in the Talmud. Jung once said to Rivkah that he interpreted Christianity (e.g., *Aion*), and "What you have to do, as a Jew, is to do the same thing with your religion." Jung's psychology is a bit Christological, even Neumann told him so. I felt that very much, too. Even though a Jungian approach opens up doors because of the ability to see symbolically, to put it solidly into a Jewish framework requires deeper knowledge of Jewish sources. That we don't have. Unfortunately we don't have it in Israel either, because Jungian psychology doesn't attract those who are well-versed in Jewish tradition and studies.

GD: We had "a second honeymoon" in Israel in 1949, and visited Israel again in 1958, before I finished the institute. I was invited to lecture at the Ahavah Institution in the town of Kiriat Bialik, on the Creation. I was introduced to Dr. Kritz, the psychiatrist of the Kupat Holim in the North. He was a Freudian, having met Freud. He said, "Freud or Jung, it doesn't matter. We need psychotherapists. You just come, and I'll give you work." My friends in Zürich told me I was naive, but I felt Dr. Kritz was sincere. When I came in 1959, I turned to him, and after a week he sent me patients, one in German, one in English, and after a month I had a full practice.

YK: I first came here in 1935. In 1937, my mother visited, and she persuaded me to come with the new grandchild to visit my parents. Then I had to find work to get back here.

Jung, the Zürich Institute and the Analysts

The present Institute is beautifully located in Küsnacht, embedded in a green garden next to the lake. Until 1978 it was located in the building that still serves the Psychology Club. The library has the characteristic smell of old books. Photos of known analysts hang on the glass-covered shelves, and there is a strange display of several photos with the heading "unknown." What does that reflect — a search for the unknown? for the missing and displaced? Or has the personal been left out? Who were they, the people inhabiting this Club and Institute at Gemeindestrasse 27 in those days?

YK: The Jung Institute started in 1948, in the building of the Jung Club. It was all very homey and informal. The seminars were held in the living room. At the first floor were the offices, with Aniela Jaffé as the secretary. The atmosphere was quite free, not like the common Swiss formality. It became like a home for us foreigners. At the beginning of the semester all the students were invited to a tea that Jung would attend. Everybody wanted to meet him. He was easy, human and quick. There was both a social and academic life in Zürich, studying together and going on hikes.

GD: It was different among the Swiss students. My first encounter with Jung was in 1949, before my studies, when my analyst invited me to come to the club. There was a special atmosphere, everyone waiting for Jung. Suddenly he came, with Ms. von

Franz and Ms. Hannah. All the ladies rushed forth, and tried to talk to him. Jung always had the same chair, like Mrs Jung and all the other analysts. The most interesting part of the lectures was when he said something in the discussion. I recall him in Eranos (scholarly lectures on spiritual themes), after a lecture of which I hadn't understood a word. In the intermission, Jung sat on the terrace and explained the lecture. In Ascona, where the lectures were held, he was really informal. However, in the Club in Zürich the atmosphere was more formal.

All the well-known analysts, who had all been analysed by Jung himself, or by Mrs Jung, lectured at the Institute. C. A. Meier, who was the first Director of the Institute, gave an excellent course on the Association experiment. Mrs Jung lectured on "The Ego and the Unconscious," Rivkah Kluger on Gilgamesh, "The Psychology of Religion," "Women in the Old Testament," "Job."

Then there was Kurt Binswanger (a cousin of the familiar Ludwig Binswanger), who gave seminars, e.g., one on homosexuality, at his home.

At the end of the year the students gave a performance. My wife played Lilianne (Frey), and Yechezkel played Dr. Binswanger.

YK: I played all the male analysts. This was the Fassnacht, the carnival. There was a masquerade, and in 1953, I played Binswanger, and James Hillman played the patient coming to him.

These parties were very nice, everyone, analysts and trainees, were together, dancing. That year Jim Hillman suggested we make a skit on the Institute. He came on as a student coming to Zürich, wanting analysis. First coming to the secretary, someone imitating Aniela Jaffé, telling his story, that he hates his father and loves his mother, a typical Oedipus problem, asking what can he do about it. 'She' then sent him to different analysts, and he would have, in the skit, an interview with each one. I played Binswanger, Meier, Bash and Riklin.

The Club had lectures every two weeks, that also Jung attended. They were given in the seminar room. At one end was a desk for the speaker, in the first rows easychairs. Jung's chair was in the second row. Because Rivkah was a member, and I was a friend of hers, I was always invited to the Club meetings. From my seat I could watch both the speaker and Jung. Preparing for the skit I would watch the analysts, to pick up their idiosyncracies. Binswanger was a very nice old gentleman. He had a habit of every once in a while brushing his hair back, and turning his neck when putting his tie in order. He was a motherly old gentleman, always smiling, saying "yes yes." In the skit I imitated his habits. After the performance he congratulated me about my good imitation. I felt very sorry, though, because later I would see how I had spoilt something for him; he would catch himself in the middle of his habit and stop.

GD: We, Lilo my wife, and myself, were very friendly with Hillman, Bob Stein and Guggenbühl.

The first Jungian congress was in 1958, attended by maybe fifty to sixty people. It was a special atmosphere. Jung, Neumann, Kirsch were there.

YK: The student organisation, AGAP, of the graduates, was organized in 1953. While today there are hundreds of members, I was one of the six charter members. The curatorium (management) got into a fury, asking us not to get incorporated, because they were just about to organize the International Organization. So we didn't incorporate ourselves legally, but we were accepted into the International Organization, which consists of all the different societies, plus AGAP.

As concerns the training, besides our reading we were expected to attend seminars, e.g., on association, dreams, fairy tales. We were orally examined, after the second year. We got graded. If not passed we could not go on to the diploma examination. There was a clear academic basis besides the analytical basis. There were cases when a student passed all the examinations but was then rejected, because the examiners/teachers (who were all analysts) had a feeling he lacked something. This actuates the countertransference in the analyst. In one such case the analyst was Mrs Jung, who fought like a tiger for someone to be accepted, but he wasn't.

Meetings with Jung

Today, especially after Andrew Samuels' Jung and the Post-Jungians, we talk about "schools" of analytical psychology - archetypal, classical, developmental. At the time, these were maybe reflections of personality as well as different theoretical orientations (e.g., Hillman vs Neumann). There must have been—just like today—differences in praxis and emphases on, for instance, personal vs archetypal, associations vs amplifications. And what was Jung like?

GD: Around 1950, I had painted a picture from a dream, in Active Imagination—something we all did, in words or painting—of a primordial animal, within which there was a godly figure. Dr. Frey said it was a very interesting archetypal picture. She showed it to Jung and brought back his comments on the picture. In 1952 or 53, I had a very archetypal dream, and Dr. Frey said, "Well, this is a dream for the boss." I got a date, and went to Küsnacht, to Jung, in a private meeting. He was very tall, peasant-like, around 78 years old. His amplification of the dream made it come alive. My analyst had told me, "Don't talk about personal material, he is only interested in the archetypal." We talked about circumcision. He said, "Well, you know, Neumann writes very naively about castration complex with regards to circumcision, and it's not like that." He enlarged on the theme, it was highly interesting. A year or so later I had one other meeting with him on an archetypal dream.

I attended a couple of candidate seminars with Jung in Küsnacht. He spoke about depression, and once he was asked by a student about becoming conscious, and he said, the more difficult thing is how time and again to become "unconscious."

I saw Dr. Frey and then went to von Franz. Everything was orthodox Jungian, all analysts were direct pupils of Jung. The difference was, that von Franz took the material and amplified. It overwhelmed me, and didn't speak to me. In control, I went to three different analysts with the same dream of one patient, and of course everyone said something else. It is one's own personal equation that one brings into the dream interpretation; it is not something objective. Jolande Jacobi, I felt, was always more Freudian, not really in the Jungian spirit, which was rather represented by Frey, von Franz and Mrs Jung.

YK: I was in simultaneous analysis with Meier and Emma Jung. We were advised to work with a man and a woman. I don't think that was very profitable; there was a lot of repetition. With Mrs Jung, it was very nice. The first time I went to the Jung house, there was, at the famous door to their house, a little chain you pulled down that rang a bell inside. Who opened the door? Jung. He was a very direct, friendly person. Upstairs was the room of Mrs Jung. Rivkah worked with him. And sometimes I would get to see Jung himself. We would talk about me, not only about a particular dream, but about the situation. One could be overwhelmed by him. But I was not. I would look at him, wonder about him. I didn't get that feeling of numinosity around him, which others have spoken about. Once I had taken a camera with me, and at the end of the interview I asked if I could take a picture of him. He said, "Yes, go ahead." Immediately he lit his pipe.

Being a critical person I looked at Jung critically, while others looked at him with numinosity. I questioned him about some things he had written.

ES: Like what?

YK: He wrote about a young man who unashamedly took advantage of an older woman, a poor teacher, because she was in love with him: he exploited her, without morals. Jung threw him out. I asked him, "Why did you throw him out? He had a problem. His lack of morality needed to be corrected. In analysis you cure the soul, and here was a soul that needed curing." I didn't get an answer.

Once Rivkah and I had dinner in the restaurant in Bollingen, overlooking the lake, with Ms. von Franz and Ms. Hannah. The owner came up to say hello; he knew them, since they, like Jung, would come there often. He spoke about Jung as "this nice old gentleman, nice old farmer," whom he would invite to sample the wines in the cellar. They would sit on the cellar steps sampling wine and talking. One time a friend of his came by and told him, "Do you know who that is? He is a world famous psychologist." After that, the restaurant owner said, something happened: "I could no longer feel so free. All of a sudden he was this big man, while before he had just been this nice farmer down the road. That's how natural he was."

GD: Jung himself tells the story how he used to play like a child in the waterflow, putting sticks into it. Once, when he raised his head he saw how the neighbour made a sign to his daughter, pointing his finger to his head that he is a bit crazy.

Jung, the Jews, Anti-semitism

It is a sign of maturity, that allegations of anti-semitism are no longer brushed under the carpet, split-off and let to "linger in the shadow." The Psychology Club in Zürich has become ill-reputed for the numerus clausus against Jews during and after the war. How sincere is the Club's search for atonement? The "Historical Lectures" series, parallell to the 13th Congress, summer 1995, started with a re-reading of James Kirsch's lecture from 1930 on "The present situation of the Jew in the world," followed by Emma Jung's on "Guilt."

And this is how the numerus clausus *is referred to in an official pamphlet on the Club's history: "Because the Club wished to remain small, membership had to be restricted in the mid-nineteen-thirties when there was an influx of foreigners to Switzerland from Nazi Germany. Many of the people who wished to join the Psychological Club were Dr. Erich Neumann's Jewish analysands. Fearing that the Swiss character of the Club would be lost with so many foreigners applying for membership, the Committeee decided to restrict the intake of foreign members by introducing a quota. ... Later on, when there were fewer applications for membership by foreigners those who were eligible to join (Jews included) were able to do so. Cancelling the quota was therefore overlooked until 1950."*

"Overlooking" sounds too soft and easy on oneself, and "fewer applications" sounds a-historical and cynical.

YK: There were several Jews around Jung. Considering his so-called anti-semitism, it is worthwhile to study the book, *Lingering Shadows — Jungians, Freudians and Anti-Semitism* (Shambhala, 1991; edited by Maidenbaum & Martin).

Why so many Jewish doctors, analysts and psychologists? There is something in the Jewish psyche that brings more Jews to study this field. It is a secular rabbinate. It is the ideal of a Jew becoming a rabbi, or a doctor; and the psychologist is a doctor of the soul. That's one reason why there are so many Jews around Jung. Secondly, Jung as a Christian was concerned with applying his psychological ideas to understand the symbolism behind Christianity and the meaning of it, which doesn't make him an anti-semite, or that his psychology is for the sake of Christianity. Because he is a believing Christian (not in the narrow sense), there is a tendency in his writings to deal with the Christian myth. That doesn't make him an anti-semite. The Jews that were close to Jung, at first, as he himself says somewhere, were assimilated Jews. He didn't learn much about Judaism from them. Freud, too, was dissociated from his Judaism to some degree. Though he absolutely was Jewish, he didn't connect to it in a feeling-full way. Religion to him is an illusion.

Bernhard, who founded the Jungian group in Italy, was a Jew, but made no use of his Jewishness. And Kirsch was a Jew but primarily a Jungian. (Gerhard) Adler in London was more consciously a Jew, but Jewishness didn't play a great role with him—psychology did.

GD: He often came to Israel, and was friendly with Neumann.

YK: Max Zeller, as well a Jew, was primarily a psychologist. His son, David, lives here in Israel. He is a rabbi. His first taste of Jewishness was when the Zeller family used to come to our house; Rivkah and I would invite them for Passover. His father, the analyst, David quips, was "an orthodox Jungian but a reformed Jew," while he, David, is "an orthodox Jew but a reformed Jungian."

Especially after reading *Lingering Shadows* it seems clear that the problem with Jung and anti-semitism started with a lecture/article in 1934* on "Psychotherapy Today."

GD: Maybe the radio interview in 1933.

YK: He speaks, in Germany, negatively about "Jewish psychology," which is not "Aryan psychology," so he sounds like a Nazi. But he wasn't a Nazi. His problem was with Freud. The break with Freud was a calamity for him. It becomes clear that he had an anti-Freud, and therefore an anti-Jewish, psychological bias. So it is there.

I remember a private dinner at friends in Los Angeles to which Barbara Hannahh had been invited. At the dinner she mentioned something about the Jews in the Psychology Club. She talked about the Jews in a disparaging way. She was obviously not aware that I was a Jew. My good friend the hostess said, "But some of my best friends are Jews!" It came out innocently. She certainly was far from being an anti-semite. Then I told Ms. Hannahh, I am a Jew. She then flustered and blustered to wriggle out of her faux pas.

GD: There are many more Jewish Freudians than Jewish Jungians, like there are many more Freudian than Jungian analysts. As you said, Yechezkel, the Jews went to study and became analysts because they are interested in the soul. When I was in America in 1951, I saw some Freudian psychiatrists, and when I talked about Jung my feeling was that they were against Jung, Jungian psychology, not only because of Freud, but because they didn't want to go deeper into themselves, in a Jungian way, so they made use of so called Jungian anti-semitism, to justify their ignorance of Jungian psychology.

About the Jewishness of Jim Hillman. He is a real American Jew, came from Atlanta. I went to Scholem once, we talked about

---

* ["Zur gegenwartigen Lage der Psychotherapie," *Zentralblatt für Psychotherapie*, 1934; An Interview on Radio Berlin with Adolf Weizsacker, June 26, 1933.]

psychology. He met Hillman in Eranos, and said to me, "He is a very bright, intelligent Jew, but he didn't make any use of his Jewishness."

YK: He became a Jungian because of Rivkah. He was passing through Zürich on his way to India. He stopped for some reason and inquired at the Jung Institute, and started analysis with Rivkah. I recently came across a card from that time, in which he writes that he is sending her a bottle of wine, "nearly as old as I am," for New Year, expressing his thanks for bringing him into Jungian psychology.

In the course of time, as often happens, the Jewish question comes up in a Jew. Hillman's grandfather translated the book of Ruth from Hebrew for the Jewish Publication Society Bible, which is the book that I wrote on. He told me this, when he came to me, on Rivkah's advice, to learn how to say Kiddush (sanctification) on Friday night. I don't know for how long he did it.

GD: He had a group of Jewish people in the 50's, even beginning of the 60's. I was invited there once.

I want to say a word on Jung's so called anti-semitism. He said in 1933-34 that there is a Jewish psychology. This is correct, but if you say it in 1934 it is bad judgment. Then there was the antisemitism, the *numerus clausus*, in the Club. Not all the Jews were allowed in. Only now, in the bulletin of the Jung Club, they had a commission investigating it. I don't know how much Jung knew about it.

YK: He knew. Sigi Hurwitz was interviewed by *Lingering Shadows* on that question. In order to join the Club you had to have two recommendations. Sigi Hurwitz was recommended by Toni Wolff and Jung. That was very pleasing for him. Jung told him that that was in spite of the fact that it goes over the quota for Jewish members. Sigi said "What!" And in that case he withdraws his application. He didn't want to belong to any organization that has a *numerus clausus*. That made Jung sit up. So he knew it. When Sigi Hurwitz reacted that way they stopped the *numerus*

clausus. To be fair, it should be added that the general membership of the Club was ignorant of the *numerus clausus*, which the
executive committee had inaugurated.

GD: But it was not revised officially until now. You told me the
story about Rivkah and Aniela (Jaffé) sitting there, not being
asked in to a discussion, before they were members. As Jews they
were not asked in.

YK: When Aniela was nominated to become a member of the
Club, there were some voices of objection because she was Jew-
ish. Jung said, "If she is not accepted I will resign from the Club."
But the *numerus clausus* was there. Rivkah was a member before
Sigi was. I don't think she knew about it. I can't imagine her,
with her Jewish soul, not reacting to it.

GD: At my time, I was admitted without any problem.

YK: During all that time, when I was there, no feeling of anti-
semitism occured to me, except from (Jolande) Jacobi.

Looking Back

*Coming of age enables one to look back, and possibly to enlarge one's
perspective on the future as well. Both Dr. Kluger and Dr. Dreifuss
have written on Jewish topics from a Jungian perspective. I asked
them what each of them feels is his particular, contribution, to which
they answered only modestly.*

GD: I have tried to bring Jungian understanding to Jewish material, not only the Bible, but the Midrash and the Agadah. My
knowledge is not enough, though. I see that as my small contribution, as well as having been teaching at the Schools of Psychotherapy in Tel Aviv and in Haifa, bringing Jungian psychology
into the profession in Israel. Once, when teaching in Tel Aviv, we
had dinner with Shalita [the founder of the School of Psychother-
apy]. It was decided to open a school of psychotherapy in Haifa. I

had good contact with her. I had once been co-speaker to a lecture of hers on empathy, from a Jungian point of view. She was open to Jungian psychology, and made me Director of Studies in Haifa. The Freudians couldn't understand this. And I have lectured for instance at the Kupat Holim Clinic in Haifa. Shamai Davidson, who was head of the clinic, used to say, "This is a case for a Jungian," second half of life, religious problems. I was also invited to Berlin giving a seminar to the German Jungians on anti-semitism and the Holocaust. It was very moving. They were young people who had to come to grips with the Nazi time, and with their parents having been Nazis.

YK: I have not been so extravertedly busy. My seminars here have mainly been on Jewish subjects. Even in the Gilgamesh seminars we had a background to Judaism; then archetypal motifs in the Bible. I have also given on the history of dreams, including how the Talmud speaks about dreams, bringing a Jewish point of view in relation to dreams. In L. A., I would give lectures, e.g., on the archetypal background of Israel today, following which a friend of Rivkah's came up and said, "That's the best piece of Zi-onist propaganda I have heard in a long time."

So it would be to try to understand what comes up in the Jew-ish psyche, from the point of view of what is pertinent to the Jew as a Jew. To correct some of the Christian Jungians, who don't know much about Judaism, and therefore sometimes can make terrible mistakes. Rivkah told me about a patient who had been working with Esther Harding. This patient had very Jewish ar-chetypal dreams, e.g., of the shofar [ram's horn]. Harding dis-missed that as primitive and not significant, not having the feeling of the numinosity of the Shofar. It needs a certain knowledge of Jewish tradition and symbolism to understand the dreams of a Jew properly. If you take a dream to three different people you get three different interpretations. It is possible that if it is a Jew-ish subject, that even though there may be some differences, they would not ignore or miss completely the Jewish meaning to cer-tain symbols.

GD: Christian analysts knew almost nothing of the Jewish development after the Bible (Midrash, Talmud or Kabalah).

As the interview came to an end, Yehezkel Kluger showed pictures of the exterior places—Zürich, Jung's home, the people who were there. I found myself getting a glimpse at the interface between the interior and the exterior of Drs. Kluger and Dreifuss as regards their involvement with Jungian psychology during the second half of this century, for which I thank them.

"Psychology— Monotheistic Or Polytheistic": Twenty-Five Years Later

James Hillman

Twenty-five years ago, in the Journal, *Spring 1971*, there appeared my article "Psychology—Monotheistic or Polytheistic?," a first attempt at revisioning depth psychology and its therapeutic practice, an attempt based upon very old, very tangled, and in some ways Florentine, roots of Western culture. That article placed the dilemmas of psychotherapy in a cosmological context prior to Freud's nineteenth-century medical positivism and to Jung's Romantic origins and influences. Yet it drew upon the same sources as they—the Greek and Roman mythic imagination, attempting to take these classical sources to their full implication by exposing the inevitable conflict of that mythical imagination with the dominant one of Western culture: that of the Bible. I referred to this conflict in the manner of usual scholarship as one between Hellenism and Hebrewism.

This paper was originally presented in April, 1996, at the Casa Machiavelli near Florence, Italy.

This essay of twenty-five years ago sought to expand the psychology of the consulting room toward philosophy and mythology on the one hand, and on the other to turn the attention of therapeutic theory backward to the basic cleft in the ground of Western culture and which Western culture straddles, the clash between pagan and Christian, that is, between the Greek, Roman, Etruscan, Carthaginian, Celtic and Germanic imagination and the imagination of the Bible—Christian, Hebrew, Mohammadhan.

Further, I began there a review of the basic idea of diagnosis, the *Krankheitsbild* or "clinical picture" in terms of cultural illness, the sickness of images in our culture, owing to the long historical prejudice against images for their association with polytheistic paganism, or in monotheistic language: "idolatry and demonism." I urged the clinician to study not only the images of sickness but also this sickness of images.

As we all know this historical conflict persisted for centuries and was never laid to rest, resurrecting in poets and painters and composers who attempted to restore the ancient myths and Gods, in folk festivals with their evident traces of Mediterranean paganism, and in the Church councils' theological controversies over images, and the trials of heretics. All this is well known. That these same issues arrive in psychological practice, that this conflict between monotheism and polytheism is fundamental to depth psychology where the old pagan forces arise again, was less well known, although Freud and Jung opened our eyes to the myths in the pathos, the Gods in the diseases. Both also wrote strongly against the unconsciousness resulting from Western religious thinking.

And, as you also know in that essay of twenty-five years ago, I tried to rejuvenate the faded awareness of that war between monotheism and polytheism by throwing myself full tilt into the battle on the side of pagan polytheism. Though an old warrior, and living in a rural retreat, unlike Cincinnatus I have not retired from warfare.

What I did not then recognize and now begin to see is that a monotheistic vision informed my own eyes when reading and interpreting the monotheistic position. In other words, I was fighting in my martial manner—intemperate, unrelenting, and blind—not as an old Roman Pagan, but with the very, almost fanatical, attitudes of what I was attacking! I was acting as a monotheist even while defending polytheism. I took the Bible—Hebrewism, Christianism—with the very literalism that I accused it of.

How would a pagan read those pages? To answer, I do not want to turn back to the Origen/Celsus arguments—largely anyway obliterated by Christian censorship—or the discussions in the Renaissance by Pico and others who tried to amalgamate and resolve in subtle ways all these differences.

Rather I want to demonstrate how we can review, revision even, fundamental Biblical tales in such a way that our method of reading and the meaning emerging from the reading happily accord with a pagan feeling. By this "pagan feeling" I mean a style that welcomes myth, personification, fantasy, complexity, and especially humor, rather than singleness of meaning that leads to dogma. Now, when we turn to the Bible it will be with an eye freshened from twenty-five years of mythical sensibility and metaphorical understanding.

II

To show you what I mean by this re-reading, let us look at four particular passages, all of them rather crucial for the Western religious traditions. For example, the Fifth Commandment (Exodus 20:12), "Honor thy Father and thy Mother." Why in the world does this appear tucked in the middle between the four great theological ordinations that come first and the societal prohibitions of the last five commandments about murder, adultery, theft, perjury, and envy?

I believe this fifth commandment is precisely placed and holds the first part and last part together. If we read the text (Deut. 5:16), this commandment establishes the personal parents as guarantors of fate. It reads: "that thy days may be prolonged and that it may go well with thee, upon the land which the Lord thy God hath given thee." The parental injunction continues the elimination of "other Gods," the local, pagan, immanent Gods of the land, and replaces them with your personal parents.

Parents have been elevated to the position of ancestor spirits: they bestow long life and protect from early death; like invisible daimones, they bear good fortune ("that it may go well with thee"); finally, like pagan nature spirits they are attached to the land, the earth belonging not to them but claimed as His, by the transcendent God above.

Once the relation with the local ancestral spirits is replaced by human parents, then a moral code for a social contract must be spelled out—the final five commandments. In a pagan world, the moral code is upheld by invisible forces, articulated in rituals. Societal order depends on the ancestors, gods and daimones and lesser animated powers who take part in human affairs and keep them in a lawful order.

In place of ritual and taboo, we are given commandments; in place of ancestor spirits, personal parents.

A narrow reading, a literal reading, sees only the reduction of the pagan protectors and bestowers of life to ordinary human parents. As well, this narrow reading sees the human parents exalted to supra-human dimensions. This cosmic position of the Father and Mother reinforced by the place of the commandment following directly upon the first theological four defining God and his worship, affects our theories of therapy to this very day. Parents are honored in every therapeutic system as the determinants of each case history. The fifth commandment thus becomes the basis of humanism and secularism and the narrowing of the idea of family to hereditary relations.

But there could be a wider, more generous reading, a pagan reading. It would say that we can find a father and a mother in all things that prolong your days, wherever things go well with thee, and parenting may be discovered in the place, the land, the earth where we inhabit. Such would be a more environmental and animistic way of honoring the Father and the Mother, and would deliver your actual parents from having to carry in their persons the exaggerated burdens of your destiny—the length of your life and its fortune.

The Second Commandment, my next example, is even more subtle to read. It seems so clearly a prohibition of the pagan mode of worship, the pagan mode of thinking in images. The text reads:

(Exodus 20:12) "Thou shalt not make unto thee a graven image, nor any manner of likeness, of anything that is in heaven above, or that is in the earth beneath, or that is in the water..."

Very clear and straight forward—no imitation of nature, no likenesses. Don't focus on nature if you are going to pay attention to God. God is very jealous of images of nature, maybe of nature itself—for in the next line, God says exactly this. Don't pay obedience to nature because I am "a jealous God."

But then this most curious event occurs. Moses comes down from the mountain "with the two tables in his hand; tables that were written on both their sides...and the tables were the work of God, and the writing was the writing of God, graven upon the tables...(Exodus 32:15)." You can see an icon of these tablets in most any synagogue anywhere. So, the very commandment that says "no graven images" is graven on an image by God himself and becomes a graven image.

Even more subtle, more perplexing: God does not ban images as such—fantasy images, dream images, the images such as Ezekiel saw. It is the graven kind, the fixed, chiseled, or what I am calling literal. God seems to warn less against images than against literalism, saying, in brief, "Don't take your images literally."

What kind of trick is God playing here?

How else read these seemingly straight directions except as strange conundrums? They present subtle twists that displace the subject and deconstruct the first literal meaning. Such twists we nowadays call "jokes" and which may be the *fons et origo* of Jewish humor.

For instance, two stories of Abraham (Genesis 17, 18 and 22): Now Abraham is the great traditional patriarch, God's most devout servant, pious, righteous, a true believer. God has to put him to the test, of course, because God doesn't seem to believe anyone—not Abraham, not Job. Anyway, God demands a demonstration of faith from Abraham. Take your little boy Isaac up the mountain and slay him for a burnt offering, showing your devotion beyond all human attachments.

Clearly what God asks doesn't make sense. The future generations would come from this son, God's whole chosen people. It's not only short-sighted, it's horrible. An atrocity. But good old

Abraham goes right along with the plan; gets up early in the morning, cuts some firewood, and goes where God told him to go. He laid the fire and bound his son upon it, and had his knife at the ready. Just as he was about to kill the boy, he was stopped by the voice of God. Lo and behold, right behind them a ram was caught in a thicket which then became the sacrificial offering.

Abraham, in his literal understanding of God's will, had to be stopped by God himself, who was, in effect, saying: Hold it, old man! Don't take me so literally. This murder of your boy is not what I meant. I want you to dedicate your son, to offer your son, recognize your son's sacrality, but not *kill* your son! You have to hear through my messages; that's why I sent the angel, to intercept you. You have to hear the *angel* in the words; the invisible *angelos*, the message, not just the literal words.

What Abraham had to give over and kill off was the thick-skulled, ram-headed quickness in his mind-set that gets caught up in the thickets of literal understanding.

The second story of Abraham shows him again needing a lesson about literalism. This story seems more to do with Sarah his wife and her conception of Isaac. They were both very, very old; and, as the text says: "It had ceased to be with Sarah after the manner of women." When God informed her that this couple, "well stricken in age," would bear a child, Sarah laughed—"After I am waxed old, shall I have pleasure, my lord being old also?"

When Abraham hears this pronouncement from God that Sarah will give birth to their child, Abraham laughed, too, and "said in his heart: 'Shall a child be born unto him that is a hundred years old?'"

Their laughter gives earnest commentators much to worry about—especially Sarah's laugh. Is it a laugh of mockery and irony and plain disbelief—like saying, 'Get on with you, God, don't be pulling my leg. Don't make fun of an old women who has no son.' Mockery as "laughing at" is how the word laugh is generally used and especially in the Gospels (Mt. 9:24; Mk. 5:40; Lk. 8:53), referring to scornful disbelief in the words and acts and prophecies of Jesus.

Or, is the laughter in Sarah already a sign of fertility? An indication of crone wisdom in her—like that of Baubo in Greece and the Oni witches in Japan? Her sexual fantasy is very much alive—speaking to God about *Edna*, "pleasure" as if it would be impossible with such an old husband. Although her natural time had passed, she had knowledge of the unnatural aspect of sexual fantasies and their procreative power. And Abraham, too, had to work through the naturalistic fallacy, the literal limits on his imagination of creativity.

The marvelous detail in this story is less the fertility marvel as such than the fact that both of them—90 and 99 as the Bible states—laughed, and produced a child. Clearly, the laughter and the fertility belong in the same image, and, note well, *laughter comes first, preceding procreation.* Laughing produced the child, and that's why its name, Isaac, derives from the Hebrew root, "to laugh." And—I draw your attention to this further exegetical particular: laughter and fertility are joined *only* in this image. No one in the whole big good book has such good laughs.

Monotheism cautions us *not* to laugh, and the words translated as laugh and laughter in both Greek and Hebrew generally mean "laugh at," deride, mock; only Eccleiastes says there is a time for laughter and that one of these times is feasting and celebration. Otherwise, Luke warns: "Woe unto you who laugh now, for ye shall mourn (6:25); and James (4:9) writes: "Be afflicted, and mourn, and weep; let your laughter be turned to mourning..."

That's about it! There is praise and jubilation, but no good laughs. No smiles either—a word for "smile" doesn't even appear! (Remember the tradition that the Greek Gods smile, especially Aphrodite, called "the smiling one.")

But Abraham and Sarah—they laugh. For them God is telling them a dirty joke, like the sort we still hear about old people and their ribald fantasies.

By the way, a little excursion for Biblical scholars who are probably anyway uncomfortable with my exegetical style. The word *edna*, translated "pleasure" in the Jewish Bible and the King James Bible, is *voluptas* in the Vulgate of Jerome. It is, however, altogether excluded, the phrase not appearing at all, in the Septuagint. Today probably, *edna, pleasure, voluptas* would be translated by French Freudian Feminists as *jouissance*, that is, if they look into that patriarchal text at all.

III

Now, with the mighty authority of the Bible to back us we may turn to the attack on literalism, my favorite enemy. I have called literalism the enemy in various writings. It is still the danger, the disease endemic to psychology. The God in this disease is monotheism—even if not the God whom the monotheists refer to, since that God, as we just saw, plays tricks and makes jokes, and tries to teach his beloved patriarch, Abraham, about multileveled understanding.

The disease of literalism comes with writing, that is, when images are graven. This is the deep prophetic implication in the second commandment: Moses, you are going to get all this written down, and therefore henceforth your followers are going to be the people of the book. Moreover, that sect coming along later known as Christians are going to write sacred books of their own, one of which announces, "In the Beginning was the Word, and the Word was with God, and the Word was God." That is, giving to the word the utmost divine omnipotent authority. (Of course, the Bible says God doesn't begin with "the word." He begins with *making distinctions* about light and dark, above and below, etc., and also with *mythical tales* about mythical places, like Eden, and mythical animals and people like Adam and Eve.

Myths have no "authorized version" as the main Protestant Bible is called in the English-reading world. Myths are best authorized on the authority of their teller. Oedipus is told by Sophocles, but also by Voltaire, Cocteau and Freud; Ulysses' wanderings by Homer, but also by extraordinary authors such as Joyce and Kazantzakis. Myth allows many versions; myth contains many versions; myth requires many versions. No *graven* images.

However, when a pagan like D. H. Lawrence tells a Jesus story embroidered with unauthorized details, or the filmmaker Martin Scorsese presents his invention of the "Last Temptation of Christ"—these versions are heresy.

An authorized version, sanctified as Holy Writ, is essential to all monotheistic literalism. Simply said: God himself speaks in the book; the book is God's word, is God in verbal form. Yet the

God we have uncovered in the two Abraham tales breaks the naturalistic fallacy of fertility, and even deconstructs his own clear instructions to Abraham by producing the ram in the thicket in place of Isaac. It would seem God is not the literalist that orthodox monotheism would wish him to be. Or, perhaps he deconstructs his own message as if he likes to joke.

IV

Lest we become too literal ourselves—always the risk in a martial discourse—let us return to smiles and laughter. For it is the laugh, a primal laugh not a primal scream, that brings together our main themes: Hebrew monotheism, Hellenic paganism and psychoanalysis.

First, we may remember that one origin of depth psychology is Freud's great Jewish joke book, one of the thickest and longest of all his treatises. Freud, however, owing to his Hebraic tradition got something backwards. He read the jokes for their instructive lesson, their secret hidden meaning. A pagan-influenced psychology reads secret hidden meanings as a joke. Not what's hidden in a joke is sexual innuendo; but hidden in sexuality is grand comedy, and which provides the stuff through the ages for comedies such as the bedroom farce. As the poet W. H. Auden wrote in his "New Year Letter" (1940):

...truth, like love and sleep, resents
Approaches that are too intense,
...through the Janus of a joke
The candid psychopompos spoke.

Sarah understood this, but Freud didn't. Yet today how we laugh at the subterfuges of Freud regarding Martha and Minna, and at the ridiculous material of those early cases and their comic figures: Little Hans, the Wolfman, Dora, Anna O., Irma's Injection. All taken so intensely by those scientifically deliberating bearded men of Vienna and the non-drinking clinicians and serious women devotees in Zürich.

The reduction of the pompous to the humorous, the conversion of the sexually hidden to a joke (rather than the joke to the
sexually hidden), is what Charles Boer and I tried to exhibit with
our own little joke, *Freud's Own Cookbook.**

That book, a seemingly simple parody of Freudianism and the
serious history of psychoanalysis, is actually an exemplary text of
the pagan view. It claims the laugh is essential to meaning, the
deepest meaning brings a smile, a laugh, and is therefore closer to
the nature of the Id and to redemption of personality from the
oppression of a laughless biblical superego than any other mode
of "becoming conscious." The Bible itself considers the laugh redemptive, as in Psalm 126: when Zion is restored then the
"mouth is filled with laughter," or as Luke says (6:21), "ye shall
laugh later," that is, in the afterlife, in heaven.

To the propositions that laughter is redemptive, that it cures
the insanity of literalism and that the God of monotheism himself
jokes, I summon evidence from an incarcerated madman, John
Percival. I reported on Percival in my 1985 Eranos lecture, "On
Paranoia."** Percival, an Anglo-Irish, practicing Christian, and
the son of a British Prime Minister, went into a religious paranoia
in the 1830's and was locked away for three years, during which
he suffered all sorts of delusions, including hearing God's instructions and commandments—like Abraham, and like Moses. He
wrote in detail about them in his diaries (London 1838-40), edited
by the eminent philosopher Gregory Bateson and published as
Percival's Narrative in 1961. Here is what Percival says:

> I suspect that many of the delusions which...insane persons la-
> bour under consist in their mistaking a figurative or a poetic
> form of speech for a literal one...the spirit speaks poetically,
> but the man understands it literally...the lunatic takes the lit-
> eral sense (270-71)...it does not follow that things seen in the
> spirit are to be practiced in the flesh. (307)

---

* James Hillman and Charles Boer, *Freud's Own Cookbook* (New York: Harper
& Row, 1985).
** James Hillman, *On Paranoia* (The Eranos Lectures Series, 8, Dallas: Spring
Publications, 1988).

As if Percival were addressing Abraham, he writes:

> Lunacy is also the mistaking of a command that is spiritual for that which is literal—a command which is mental for one that is physical...the intention was...not practically to put the words in execution. (279)

As his cure progressed, he "obeyed the spirit of humour" because "the Deity...often intimates his will by jesting..." We may let revelations, epiphanies, prophecies, daimons descend without believing, or disbelieving, them. *Serio ludere*, said the Renaissance maxim.

Reflecting upon his three years in the madhouse, Percival presents at the end of his narrative his theory of lunacy:

> I conceive therefore that lunacy is also a state of confusion of understanding, by which the mind mistakes the commands of a spirit of humour, or of irony, or of drollery; ... that, perhaps, this is the state of every human mind.... I mean that in the operations of the human intellect, the Deity...often intimates his will by thus jesting...that in the misapprehending or perverting of this form of address may consist original sin.

The original sin, then, is not the fall from grace owing to what the Church Fathers called "the animal mode of generation" and what Freud called the libidinal Id that is universally basic to human nature. Rather the Fall is the fall from metaphor, the fall into literalism. The Paradise lost is the loss of the sense of humor so that you are no longer able to get God's jokes. As Percival's cure progressed, he said he "obeyed the spirit of humor," whereas while he was deluded he was obeying the will and word of God. *Fiat mihi*. I believe Percival not only was cured, but converted. I think he came out of the asylum with a pagan mind.

V

All along this morning I have been using the word "pagan" quite freely. I like the word for my own self-referent reasons—and it offers us another joke: One meaning of *pagos* in

Sophocles and Euripedes is "rocky hill"; *paganos*, people of the rocky hilly countryside. A pagan is therefore a hill-man.

The Latin *paganus* was used originally in several ways: to refer to native peoples who were civilians and peasants and not members of an alien army. "Pagan" was used in distinction to others, particularly to the *alieni*, that is, members of foreign militia who came into native villages and towns throughout the Roman world, armies composed of Mithraic and mainly Christian soldiers.

Authorities seem to agree that the term *pagani* referred simply to the people *of a place*, both town people and country people who preserved their customs. *Pagani* were contrasted with *alieni*, the people from *elsewhere*. These were more likely soldiers, Roman administrators, Christians. Paganism in the ancient world can be defined as the religion of a localized homeland, which therefore accounts for the great diversity among pagan cults, customs and myths.

This basic meaning—"people of the place"—opens one more radical distinction between the two cosmoi we are contrasting. The pagan mind will not submit easily to abstract universals, the logics of science, of mathematics, to general laws. It would find alien the idea of a one, true, and universal religion as the Roman Church has defined itself.

It would be alienated by the placelessness of virtual reality and cyberspace, an internet of websites that is not actually sited, anywhere local and physical, and whose images are not attached to or framed by an environment. The pagan, as I understand its psychology, abjures universals altogether including nationalism and ecumenicalism, unless they be qualified by the particular place where the universals are effective. That's why the ancient Gods and Goddesses were always place-specific, with epithets that located them and brought out their specific local qualities. The Artemis or Hermes or Apollo of one place was not the same Artemis and Hermes and Apollo of another. Hence, "a diversity of pagan practices and beliefs."

Therefore it is so difficult to translate lectures such as this because translation not only raises the question of languages, but of transferring a mind and a soul from one place to another. All translations are traitorous and treacherous, because they assume what is said in one place can be said anywhere. The Christian missionaries taking the one true word to tribes around the world found they had to compromise the universality of their creed to accord with "the people of the place."

The logic of monotheism attempts to override place. This logic favors a cosmos of space and time, the cosmos of Decartes and Newton and Kant, a single and empty abstraction that can contain all things. The differences among things are merely differences of motions and coordinates. Places, like everything else—tastes, smells, colors that qualify the world—are only "subjective," not inherent in things, but given to them by humans. As Immanuel Kant, the most influential of all modern universalists, said, "The taste of the wine does not belong to the wine but to...the subject that tastes it." Tell that to a Tuscan *contadino*, Immanuel!

This devastation of the world as a sensory living body and the reduction of place to vast and unqualified space has led us to the architectural and ecological catastrophes we now suffer. A world that is sheer *res extensa*, of course obliterates pagans, "the people of the place," and so we find peoples fighting for place with insane passion, as in Ireland, Kurdistan, Palestine, Yugoslavia, and in the Sudan and Timor where war between polytheism and monotheism has killed perhaps a million people.

The definition of pagan as people of place, as defenders of place against the alienation brought by monotheism, explains to me—twenty-five years later—how and why my work has turned so actively to environmental, ecological and urban concerns. It is the logical outcome of my pagan disposition. Environmentalism is simply paganism in today's world. The active defense of particular sites, the localism, the championing of rivers and forests, the protection of animals and tribes against intruders from universal corporations and abstractions of government—all this is paganism in contemporary dress. The Greens and the Environmentalists will die for a dolphin or a tree. This is religion, even if without the old Gods.

It would be more conventional to regard my ecological concerns of the last five years as a return to the world after the descent into the nether regions, and the burning of the bridge to the dayworld with which I opened my book, *The Dream and the Underworld*.* This would be a Jungian reading of my ecological turn. After the *nekyia*, the introversion; the psyche moves out to the "other." But this explains a human life in terms of a developmental formula in accordance with the path of individuation. Is this not a monotheistic reading? A reading that puts us all on the same one path—first half of life, second half; inward follows outward and vice versa; compensation.

Rather, my polytheism belongs to my character as a hill-man, a pagan. My earliest excitement in philosophy came from reading Plato at Trinity University in Dublin and Plotinus at the University of Zürich, and from the overwhelming emotional impact that the physical places of Greece and Sicily had on me, unlike any I have felt anywhere including the Himalayas or Jerusalem. It was never hard for me to sympathize with Freud in regard to his pathological incident on the Acropolis, and with Jung's fainting at the Zürich railroad station intending to go to Rome, to which he never came. Particular places have singular spirits, and they call us.

The particular spirit that calls us in this place (Florence) is that of Machiavelli. He speaks directly to the martial tone with which I opened this discourse, promulgating strife between monotheism and polytheism. Machiavelli, sardonic or sincere, we cannot know for sure, said, "A prince should not have any purpose or thought...other than war." (*The Prince*, XIV)

The war that has lasted through the ages need not be understood literally, nor Machiavelli, either. I read him and understand war in the sense of Heraclitus, who said "War is the father of all things." It generates heat, focuses attention, stimulates passion, activates ideals.

By thus charging the atmosphere, Mars draws forth Mars' companion Venus, who softens the edges, that sweeter yielding which allows us to see in the Christian John Percival a pagan understanding of God and to find, in the Sufi songs and verses and

---

* James Hillman, *The Dream and the Underworld* (New York: Harper & Row, 1979).

cosmologies and in Kabbalist expositions and midrashes of Jewish monotheism, a polysemous multilayered diversity of images, metaphors, daimones and personifications that are quite pagan.

We should remember in regard to this Mohammedan and Jewish diversity that place plays a definite role. Diversity of understanding derives from diversity of place—the Mullahs are identified by Cairo or Cordoba or Baghdad and the Rabbis by Safed or Gerona or Minsk, a local school that gives the reading of the Koran a distinct flavor, much as the therapy school of Vienna differs from the school of Zurich, though both are reading the same text, the psyche.

Despite my caveat against taking war too literally and my appeal to Venus, we must never cease playing this "mono-poly" game, for the mind is always in danger of succumbing to philosophies of oneness and to the tyranny of unification in every sort of sphere. Therefore the pagan perspective will always keep diversity in mind, and with it the devotion to places, their spirits and daimones, the singularity of colors and smell, the taste of the wine and the sound of the speech of each distinct locality. For it does not matter to which Church we go, to which God we kneel, or none at all, or how we imagine the next world, so long as we do not neglect the sensate diversity of this world and the local Gods who inhabit it, who bless it with flavor and color, a delight to the eyes in spring and the nose's joy, this incredible richness of each local springtime, restoring us for a short season to Eden—the *eden* that is directly related to *edna*, that Hebrew word for Sarah's "pleasure."

YOUTHFUL ILLUSION

SHEILA GRIMALDI-CRAIG

Hayao Kawai, *Buddhism and the Art of Psychotherapy.* College Station: Texas A&M UP, 1996. Pp. 184. $22.95, cloth.

D uring the recent earthquake in Kobe, Japan, Westerners were surprised that there was no looting, despite the fact that nearly everyone involved was deprived of food and material goods. Order was maintained without incident. Westerners commented on the Japanese "power of endurance." It had long been a cliché of Western psychology that "Japanese people will commit suicide more often than Westerners, because of their relatively weak egos," as Hayao Kawai reminds us in this autobiographical exploration of the Japanese psyche. But in the Kobe disaster they were well-behaved masters of their fate, where their Western equivalents would customarily have been, to put it mildly, "shaken." Indeed, in the recent TWA crash off Long Island teams of therapists and psychological counselors were dispatched immediately to comfort the families of victims, and later, teams of therapists were further dispatched to counsel the divers who were fishing up the bodies from the Sound. And lest we think this is all merely some new American indulgence, the French had their own teams of airport-crisis psychologists at the ready in Paris to console the grieving on their side.

Sheila Grimaldi-Craig taught for many years in the Connecticut Public Schools. She is the regular book reviewer for this journal.

Buddhism and the Art of Psychotherapy is not aimed at the new Western phenomenon of "victim" psychology (although as one reads this book the comparisons keep striking the reader). It is far more personal than that: Hayao Kawai was the first Jungian psychoanalyst in Japan (there are now thirteen more), having returned there after finishing his training in Zürich in 1965. This book is his take on how Jungian psychology works in a culture that is bedrock Buddhist ("Am I a Buddhist and/or a Jungian?" he keeps asking himself) and how his own professional and private life were shaped by the combination.

I doubt if there is a single *Spring* reader who has not at some point in youth had a flirtation with Buddhism. When I was growing up, in the 1950s, Zen Buddhism was the manifest antidote to American materialist crassness and Eisenhower vulgarity. You went to the works of D. T. Suzuki if you were really serious and committed, to the works of Alan Watts if you were only flirting with it, and to the Beat poems of Gary Snyder (fresh from his training in a Kyoto monastery) no matter what you were. Buddhism, which saw the world as illusion, was our greatest youthful illusion.

The reality of Buddhism, for people like the Japanese, is, as Kawai testifies, something else. It is why they do not crack when the earth opens up or the bombs come raining down. They really have, he insists, a different kind of ego.

> Here, as elsewhere, the Japanese form of ego is the focal issue. This ego has the premise of connection with others. However, I is not about the relationship of an independent ego to others. It is instead a pervasive sort of connection that exists before the ego state, a connection in which the participants share mutually the deep 'empty' world. As long as a person holds such a sense of interconnectedness, one's total vulnerability is exposed. The immense problem is that the existing world, which is the foundation of interconnectedness, is described as 'empty' or 'nothing,' and at the same time as an infinite, 'non-empty' world.

The Japanese, Kawai argues, subordinate the ego to something transcendent; they want to sacrifice ego for *something*. But of

course if that *something* is literal *nothingness*, "egocide" (as Kawai
calls it) can easily be mistaken for suicide. Kawai's patients are
always coming to him saying, "I want to die" as if they were saying only something as simple as "Good morning." He sometimes
gets so frustrated by this phenomenon that he tells them to go
ahead and do it! But then the Western-trained Kawai remembers
his Buddhism and realizes that by saying "I want to die" the Japanese patient is only doing what he is supposed to do, trying to
kill the ego in order to get closer to the world of others, which,
ironically, is the world of emptiness.

> At first, I did not understand the above issues. Therefore, I was
> trying to prevent client suicide by a Western-style ego-to-ego
> connection. As a result, I was exhausting myself and still not
> getting a positive outcome. I should have put my effort into the
> relationship of my ego and Emptiness, a vertical relationship,
> instead of into the horizontal ego-ego (client-therapist) relation-
> ship. Since these experiences, my attitude has changed a great
> deal.

There have, of course, been other books on the Jungian-
Buddhist experience * and Kawai himself has written the definitive book** on the Japanese psyche itself (which now comes with
an introduction from Gary Snyder!). But what *Buddhism and the
Art of Psychotherapy* tries to do is present Kawai's *own* approach
to psychotherapy as a result of his own experiences in this hybrid
role. It is the method of this "I" (a good Buddhist at least sometimes, he puts himself in quotation marks) that the book represents. And lest we think this is solipsistic, he reminds us that both
Jung and Freud developed their own methods out of their own
self-analyses.

---

* Mokusen Miyuki, who is both a Jungian analyst and a Buddhist priest, wrote,
with J. Marvin Spiegelman, a book which Kawai himself recommends, *Buddhism and Jungian Psychology*, Phoenix, Ariz.: Falcon Press, 1985.
** Hayao Kawai, *The Japanese Psyche: Major Motifs in the Fairy Tales of Japan*, 2nd
ed., Woodstock, Conn.: Spring Publications, 1996. This is Kawai's first book
written in English, and in many ways remains the more important, I think. It is
a study of why the female figure as it recurs in Japanese myths best expresses the
culture's ego and the country's possible future.

As Kawai grew up, he found himself rejecting Buddhism, which he says is for most Japanese merely a matter of historical background, not functioning religion. When he first entered the United States, he hesitated for a long time over the space on the visa form that asked his religion, and finally wrote "Buddhist." Part of his hesitation was the realization ever since childhood that he was "unenlightened," especially when it came to such subjects as death, which Buddhists learn to master as "nothing." Kawai admits that from childhood to the present he is still very much afraid of death.

During his adolescence, when Japan was recruiting soldiers for World War II with a no-fear-of-death die-for-the-fatherland Buddhism, Kawai felt even more alienated. When Japan was defeated in 1945, he was seventeen and beginning to reject all things Japanese, forming instead an attraction to Western art and literature. "I liked virtually everything Western," he writes, "while Japanese things seemed irrational to me. They seemed to pull me down into darkness when I was trying to get the blessing of sunlight into my life."

Yearning for Western rationalism, he studied mathematics and became a high school math teacher. "I was close to embracing science as almighty. From this perspective, I looked down on Buddhist teaching as hardly worth anyone's attention." Young Japanese intellectuals, he says, were drawn to materialism, and especially to Communism, as the solution to their post-war shock. Kawai's high school students kept coming to him with their problems, so he took a graduate course in clinical psychology at Kyoto University in order to learn how to help. He soon learned, however, that no one there had any idea of the subject. Before long, he gave up his high school teaching and himself began giving lectures on psychology at the university.

In 1959, he was given a Fulbright Fellowship to become a graduate student in psychology at UCLA. Only now for the first time did he learn of the ideas of Jung, when he took a course in the Rorschach technique from Bruno Klopfer, a Jungian analyst. Kawai then became an analytical patient of J. Marvin Spiegelman. From the outset, however, Kawai was doing all this as a matter of science, of *anti-Buddhist* science, wanting to learn the Western way of psychology. He was a difficult patient.

> At the beginning of my analysis, I was very surprised to hear the analyst, Dr. Spiegelman, say that we were going to do dream analysis. I immediately protested, saying, "I cannot trust such an irrational thing! How could I believe in 'dream messages' when I came here to study Western rationalism?" I simply could not believe anything so unscientific.
>
> My analyst responded, "Have you ever studied your dreams—what they mean?"
>
> "No," I answered.
>
> "Don't you think it's rather unscientific to disparage their study when you have not even inspected your dreams?"
>
> I thought that that made sense.

During one of his analytic sessions, Dr. Spiegelman showed Kawai the "Ten Oxherding Pictures" from the Zen tradition, pictures which illustrated the state of Buddhist enlightenment as being a process. "What a shame that I had never even known that such pictures existed in the East!" he writes. He began a study of Japanese mythology, fired now precisely by his earlier rejection of all things Japanese.

There were many problems. At the Jung Institute in Zürich, where he then proceeded to deepen his Jungian orientation, Kawai analyzed with C. A. Meier, who kept insisting that it was only natural for a Japanese man to study his Japanese roots. But his other analyst, Lilian Frey, was a woman, and Kawai had been raised in the Japanese tradition of "the man, honored; the woman, subordinated." He felt resistance to acknowledging a woman in this role over him. Then he had a dream of Frey as the sun goddess, Ameratsu, the most important figure in Japanese mythology. She replied, "I am not a goddess nor the sun. I'm simply a human being. That sun goddess exists in you."

His reaction to this was again ambivalent: on the one hand, he thought it sounded like a reasonable answer. On the other hand, he still had a strong negative feeling to Japanese mythology. It was what he calls "the Japanese attitude of relatedness" getting to him again, " in which one side cannot make a proposal without considering the ramifications for the other." Nonetheless, the dream of the sun goddess, Ameratsu, became the subject of his thesis for certification at the Institute.

But Kawai's adventures in the realm of Zürich psychology did not end there. At his final exam at the Institute, he was asked, "What are examples of symbols of the Self?" He was supposed to answer, he says, "the mandala," or one of the other official responses of the program. But suddenly, remembering the Japanese expression, "Grass, tree, country, land—all become Buddha," he replied, "Everything!"

It was hardly what the examiner wanted to ear. A heated discussion followed, in which Kawai defended his answer against the examiner's textbook. He was flunked. He doesn't tell what happened next, referring to "various difficulties." But eventually he passed and was certified, though certainly he was a first of his kind.

"Strictly speaking," he writes, "according to this Buddhist idea, the 'everything' which I affirmed was most assuredly Self-itself. There is no concept of a symbol of Self." In *Buddhism and the Art of Psychotherapy*, he discusses in detail the significance of this difference in Japanese and Western psychology.

He no sooner returned to Japan to begin his psychoanalytical practice than he realized it was not going to be easy to learn everything all over again from a Japanese point of view. For example, a patient who refused to engage in the sandplay therapy that Kawai had adapted from the Japanese tradition of *bonkei* (tray scenes) and *hako niwa* (small sandbox gardens), was asked why she refused.

> "I don't want to be cured," she said. "I'm not coming here to be cured."
> "Then why are you here?" I asked.
> "I come here just to come here."

Try dealing with that, you Western healers!

Kawai inevitably, if reluctantly, turned to Buddhist sources to enlighten his Jungianism. Of these, the dreams of a twelfth-century Buddhist monk named Myoe were particularly useful.

Throughout this re-education into Buddhism, he asks himself a continuing question: what is a Jungian? His answer is the most refreshing and cogent definition of the beast that I have ever heard:

> ...if there is a person who thinks that being a Jungian means following completely what C. G. Jung said, taking that as entirely correct, then surely I am not a Jungian. On the other hand, if a Jungian is simply one who follows her or his own individuation process, then one is a Jungian no matter what one does, as long as one stays on track. But this seems a bit too easy, too simplistic. I would say that you are a Jungian when, in order to avoid your own arbitrariness or self-indulgent living, you choose C. G. Jung as a reference point for your self-examination, in which you challenge completely your beliefs and methods and find positive meaning in doing that. When you stop finding meaning in that, then I think you would stop being a Jungian. "Jungian" means, not following Jung completely, but finding the positive meaning in confronting Jung and in rigorously comparing his approach with yours.

All this is only a preliminary to the main exposition of this book, which is a discussion of the "Ten Oxherding Pictures," a series of Japanese illustrations of the steps to enlightenment. The pictures ("Searching for the Ox," "Catching the Ox," "Coming Home on the Ox's Back," etc.) are included, along with Kawai's fascinating discussion of why the Ox is *not* the Self. These pictures are then contrasted with the *Rosarium Philosophorum* pictures of alchemy in Jung's *Psychology of Transference*. They are remarkably similar, except that in the Japanese pictures there is, at least at first viewing, no portrayal of the feminine. Kawai offers a brilliant analysis of the differences. (A modern Japanese woman has wonderfully added five new pictures of her own to the traditional Ten Oxherding Pictures, and Kawai, analyzes these as well.)

With all this as background, he concludes the book with two chapters that get to the heart of the Japanese/Jungian perspective: "What Is I?" considers the Japanese wish for "egocide," and "Personal and Impersonal Relationships In Psychotherapy," contrasts with his own Jungian one the Rogerian theory of "nondirective" psychotherapy that was prevalent in Japan when Kawai began his practice.

Throughout the book as well, almost anecdotally, Kawai takes us on excursions into some surprising cultural differences: why Japanese school children have a great phobia about going to school (while in the West we are always comparing our "lazy" students to the industrious Japanese!), why Japanese analysts have to "mother" their patients, why the Japanese find it very hard to pay an analyst for just talking, what Kawai learned from Myoe's dream diary, how in the Japanese version of the Oedipus myth, Oedipus tries to kill his mother, and so on.

But what makes this book so forceful and readable, from beginning to end, is that Hayao Kawai has written it all, and tells it all, from the perspective of his own experience, both as an analyst and as a Japanese man who rejected Buddhism and then returned to make his own Jungian peace with it. When you consider both ends of these traditions, and realize how unlikely it is for a truly autobiographical book to come out of either of them, you will appreciate what Kawai is offering here.

Get out your best Mikasa and pour yourself a cup of tea, dear reader. This is a good one.

BOOK REVIEWS

Piero Camporesi. *Juice of Life: The Symbolic and Magic Significance of Blood.* With a Foreword by Umberto Eco. Tr. Robert R. Barr. New York: Continuum, 1995. Pp. 139. Cloth, $17.95.

Every few years a book comes out of Italy that speaks as if we are still living in the wonderfully phantasmagoric studio of Marsilio Ficino's Renaissance, still plotting in the alchemical thinktank of Giordano Bruno, our bodies envisioned as strangely incomprehensible contraptions that the Galen-Hippocratic tradition of western medicine has still only barely even touched. Camporesi, who is a Professor of Italian Literature at the University of Bologna, is one of those delightfully ancient-minded Italians, like Umberto Eco himself, who introduces this book. Roberto Calasso is on the same beam. The grandfather of all of them was, perhaps, Italo Calvino. Italy is so fortunate—as France most singly is not— that it didn't lose *all* its Renaissance imaginative faculties when realism/modernism/marxism moved in. Publishers like to blurb this sort of book as "poetic" but it isn't poetry at all, it's an ancient way of imagining that got clobbered in the twentieth century in all but the most offbeat places (Lampedusa's Sicily, is probably a richer vein than even Eco's own Bologna, but let us not forget Alfred Ziegler's Zürich, or for that matter, everybody's Ascona, Switzerland right up to the present).

How else do you explain this riveting rhapsody on blood (*blood!*) that can make you laugh even as it gives you the creeps?

"Quintessences of blood, sperm, and marrow, of cock and bull testicles, were the basic elements of the elixirs of long life. Physicians, apothecaries, charlatans, and great intellectuals all agreed: the blood of a fresh, delicate man, one well-tempered in his humors, someone young, soft, and blooming with red, 'bloody' fat—a fleshy man, of a 'jovial' temperament and 'cordial' character, preferably having red hair (by association of the color of hair with that of blood)—enjoyed the indisputable primacy when it came to the slowing of the aging process. The paradoxical, esoteric myth of the *paedogeron*—the paradoxical mask of the *puer-senex* of Platonist Orphism—sprang to life again, on the level of the masses, in the unbridled quest, if not for eternal youth, at least for the elixir of long life that would make it possible to recover time gone by and consumed years, stretching across the wrinkled, shriveled countenance of age the warm, moist veil of youth. If the Faustian dream that gleamed in the conjurations of alchemical magic was everlastingly frustrated, the contrary process—the precocious aging of the very young, wasted away by dysentery to wrinkled, decrepit masks, disguising a poor, watery blood, the living paradox of the hundred-year-old baby become sheer reality, with its wrinkled, jowled face like a monkey's (in the region of Modena, this sad phenomenon, provoked by nutritional deficiencies, was called 'monkey sickness')—was before everyone's eyes. It is difficult to say to what extent the fear of this untimely, utterly precocious metamorphosis into a person of advanced age fueled the flights to ultraterrestrial paradises in which one's skin, fresh and unscathed by time, hunger or malady, would come to be washed in the dew of an incorruptible blood, and the whole body steeped in perfectly tempered and balanced humors, as in the times of the golden age, the age of peerless blood."

Or this passage on marriage:

"In this dimension of an on-going putrefactive threat, and of humoral corruption ('to a healthy, well-composed person are assigned eight pounds of blood, four of phlegm, two of choler [yellow bile], one of melancholy [black bile]'), even marriage ('communio sanguis et thori,' communion of blood and couch) becomes one of 'the most wonderful tools' of the 'human factory,' and copula a purge, a salutary 'scouring.'"

"It is well to marry early...as we learn from the fact that it produces lightness of body, ease in breathing, and cheerfulness of spirit. For, in a well-fed body, a great abundance of the last and eighth nutrient...is transformed into semen, which, except it be duly evacuated, perniciously corrupts, causing a person great trouble, and presently reducing him to emaciation and senility. If evacuated as is fitting, just as it has weighed on a person before, so after it has emerged it lightens and cheers him with its great contentment." (A. Petronio, *Del vivere delli Romani et del conservare la sanita*. 1592)

✠ ✠ ✠

Maud W. Gleason. *Making Men: Sophists and Self-Presentation in Ancient Rome*. Princeton: Princeton UP, 1995. Pp. 194. Cloth, price not listed.

In Greece under Roman occupation, public speaking became a special kind of self-presentation, one in which you showed off your education to your mostly uneducated mass audience. It was a strenuous task. You had to project your unamplified voice out over the often jeering crowd, always keeping it perfectly modulated and controlled so that you looked and sounded like the great man you were pretending to be. But what if, like Favorinus, one of the most famous orators of the day, you were a eunuch born without testicles, and your voice was a high-pitched squeak? Favorinus called his mode of speaking "the singing style" and it was wildly popular with his audiences. To many classicists, from Gibbon's *Decline and Fall* to Wilamowitz-Moellendorff, the rhetoricians of the Second Sophistic, as this period is called, were perfect examples of just how "sick" the Roman Empire became before its fall. But not to Maud Gleason, who teaches Classics at Stanford University, and who sees in these great sophists and declaimers an embodiment of "the rhetoric of manhood" itself. In the case of Favorinus, who somehow managed "to combine the charm of a certain feminine softness with the articulate dignity of a man," even his contemporaries were forced to interpret his highly elaborate self-presentation as a new phenomenon.

"Because rhetorical skill was considered a definitive test of masculine excellence, issues of rhetorical style and self-presentation easily became gendered. We find issues of power debated as if they were issues of gender. Gender is, after all, a primary source of the metaphorical language with which power relationships are articulated, in our own time as in antiquity. In the high-stakes game of self-presentation among articulate upper-class males, ways had to be found to define losers as well as winners. There had to be a hierarchy within the population of eligible competitors, a language in which comparative assessments could be made. This environment fostered the practice of skewering one's opponents for their effeminate style. It was a polemic that had nothing to do with women, who had no place whatever in this performance culture. So absent indeed were real women that the 'other,' an apparently essential component in the process of self-fashioning, had to be called into being within an entirely masculine context. Thus polarized distinctions (smooth/hirsute, high voice/low voice, pantherlike/leonine) that purport to characterize the gulf between men and women instead divided the male sex into legitimate and illegitimate players. For individuals, these stereotypes facilitated a process by which the self became exteriorized through certain highly stylized forms of self-display."

✠ ✠ ✠

Eugene Taylor. *William James On Consciousness Beyond the Margin*. Princeton: Princeton UP, 1996. Pp. 232. Cloth, $35.

In 1894, when Massachusetts, in an attempt to ban "mental healers," proposed a law that would have required all persons practicing medicine in the state "without reputable degrees" to take exams and get licensed (the exams to be given by already licensed

M.D.s), William James, America's first and greatest psychologist, protested. James was the first American to teach psychology scientifically (rather than merely philosophically), the first to set up a lab for student instruction (at Harvard), the first to grant a Ph.D. in the new subject (to G. Stanley Hall in 1878), and the author of a world-famous textbook (America's first), *The Principles of Psychology.* The legislature, impressed by the protestor, amended the bill to say only that unlicensed people could not use the letters M.D. after their names, but they did not have to get licensed or take exams to practice medicine. As a result of his championing of the mental healers (who held that morbid symptoms were the result of unconscious fixed ideas), James' reputation sank among his fellow psychologists, who viewed him as no longer a "scientist."

Eugene Taylor documents with unprecedented detail the story of James's transformation from a neurophysiological scientist to a new kind of psychologist, one for whom the depths of the psyche itself were suddenly beginning to open up:

"James's point was that if psychology truly wanted to influence character development, then it had to acknowledge that there was, in fact, a growth-oriented dimension within the normal personality to which one could make appeal and through which ideas could have an effect. The nature of this dimension, he said, was unfathomable. At its farthest reaches, we cannot say what it is; we can only say 'it is *that*.'"

⌘ ⌘ ⌘

Otto Rank. *A Psychology of Difference: The American Lectures.* Ed. Robert Kramer, with a foreword by Rollo May. Princeton: Princeton UP, 1996. Pp. 296. Cloth, $39.50.

In 1924, when Otto Rank, the most filial of Freud's disciples, published *The Trauma of Birth* (fifteen years after his book, *The Myth of the Birth of the Hero*, to which Freud himself contributed a section on "the family romance"), it was viewed by Freud and the inner circle as another major blow to "the cause" ("*die Sache*," as Freud liked to refer to psychoanalysis.) Rank argued that a child's positive and negative feelings are really directed to the mother, not the father. Birth trauma was more important than the Oedipus complex.

Rank's book appeared at a critical time in the life of his master. Freud, a year before, had started a series of painful operations for cancer of the jaw, and suspecting the worst, asked his doctor for help "to disappear from this world with decency," only to suddenly remember that his "dear" mother, Amalie, was still alive at 87. "It would not be easy to do that to the old lady," he said, and proceeded to put up with the agonies of a mouth prosthesis ("a monster," he called it) and years of acute suffering. There was an almost ridiculous magic to Freud; it was so powerful that everything that ever happened to him was seen, and continues to be seen, as a catalyst for the theories of his associates. (In this case, Rank is supposed to be saying that Freud's negative mother was the germ of this theory.)

Nonetheless, Rank, always said to be closer to Freud than Freud's own sons, was now up against the mother of all Catch 22s. The secret ringholders (Freud's committee for the furtherance of the cause, led especially by Karl Abraham, all of whom had been given these symbolic tokens) saw Rank's birth trauma stuff as nothing but one more unconscious flight from the Oedipus complex on the part of a disciple, for any theories that challenged Father Freud were by definition merely refusing to face the all-encompassing Oedipus complex. Freud soon concurred.

Abraham, whom Robert Kramer describes in his brilliant introduction to this book as "the keen-eyed Abraham, who had smoked out Jung from his anti-Oedipal layer long before Freud was forced to recognize the malefactor," is only one of the authority figures out to get the young Rank. Rank soon moved to the United States, where he started giving the lectures which comprise this book. In 1930, in a lecture in Washington, he told the large international audience, "I am no longer trying to prove that Freud was wrong and I am right...It is not a question of whose interpretation is correct—because there is no such thing as *the* interpretation or only *one* psychological truth." The American Psychoanalytic Association, on a motion by its president, A. A. Brill, and seconded by its vice-president, Harry Stack Sullivan, immediately removed Rank's name from its list of honorary members.

Otto Rank (1884-1939) went on to become a foremost analyst of artists (Anais Nin and Henry Miller were two of his patients). "Rank saw analysts," Kramer says, "as artists, who *use* the patient—an artiste manqué—as a living object onto whom they project their own creative urge." And neurosis itself, Rank said, in a lecture given, suitably enough, to a California audience, was but "a failure of creativity." Psychotherapy would never be the same.

"...To the Oedipus complex—which, as I said, represents the first revolt by the child against subjection of his ego by parents—we must contrast the parental complex, which we could designate, best of all, as the *Prometheus complex*. In our own emotional life, this Prometheus complex is as important as the Oedipus complex, if not more important. Whereas the Oedipus complex is founded on identification, indeed—at least in the meaning of psychoanalysis—symbolizes identification, the Prometheus complex is not only the symbol of the need or desire to create but also arises in the individual creatively, that is, spontaneously, at a crucial point, and *not* in identification with parents." ("The Prometheus Complex," 1927)

❊ ❊ ❊

The Wedding. Photographs by Nick Waplington. New York: Aperture, 1996. Cloth, $40.

Leave it to Aperture, the world's foremost publisher of photography, to send us a book of wedding pictures just in time for our "Marriage" issue. And what a wedding it was! Waplington's first book, *Living Room* (Aperture, 1991) captured the scene in the living-room of Janet and her then-partner Dave, and their four kids, in a municipal housing project in Nottingham, England. Now it's 1993, and Janet's getting married again, this time to Clive. We see them getting ready for the Big Day (shots of babies crawling around the floor or crying, Janet sitting on the floor eating an ice cream cone, kids eating potato chips while some woman lies on a couch looking sick, Clive having a beer, a diaper being changed, pizza time, Janet, all 300 pounds of her, wrapped in a towel, ironing something, some guy with a bandaged eye smoking in the kitchen), then the Big Day itself (at the Marriage Parties' Waiting Hall, the kids attacking a table of wedding party food, Janet isolated in her white wedding dress for a moment looking a little forlorn as a spaced-out guy watching her lifts a beer bottle to his lips, a two-year-old boy drinks a can of beer sitting on the floor, a morose-looking teen-ager, in dirty jeans and T-shirt, wedges himself into a corner between a television set and a wall next to Janet's wedding bouquet and drinks a beer, Janet lying on the couch barefoot and in shorts looking exhausted as Clive holds her while another kid does a backward somersault in the foreground, Janet and Clive in bed under a blanket while Clive smokes and the children keep bothering them with questions.

Irvine Welsh, author of the recent drug-dreary book/movie, *Trainspotting*, writes a humorless Postscript to the book in which he rails against "some members of the middle class [who] fail to comprehend..." and how "the Labour-controlled Nottingham Council deemed a photography exhibition in the city of Nick's *Living Room* work as not politically correct..." and "The tendency of the rich has generally been to pontificate and judge the poor based on their consumption patterns. Every can of lager lying around, every full ashtray, every television set with a color picture, every new garment is seen as an indictment..." and "...against the long-standing but totally impotent clucking, cooing, and collusion of the new puritan, liberal middle-classes, we more than ever need the fearless and empathetic voice of the acid-house generation."

Sure we do.

Now that we've re-visioned marriages, it's time to turn our attention to the stuff in which we really want to indulge—the love affairs that mark our lives forever. Jan Bauer explores "marvelous disasters;" the betrayals, taboos and excesses of impossible love. Before you reach for Ben & Jerry's Chocolate Fudge Brownie Ice Cream, read *Impossible Love: Why the Heart Must Go Wrong*. Jan examines the erotic structures of irresistible attraction with delicious love stories of the classic past and the lives of people today. (We've all been there, and remember hell fondly.)

Archetypal Sex: SPRING 57 brings together some of the hottest writers in the new post-Jungian world for an ecstatic plunge into the sexual issues of the moment—from pornography to transexualism, from unusual Haitian sex goddesses to just plain cute little tricksters. *Archetypal Sex*—you may have been doing it without ever knowing it!

Therapy, erotic and sexual? John Haule, Ph.D., a distinguished Jungian analyst, explores the steamier aspect of soul work, "necessarily a very erotic enterprise." If you are an analyst, counselor or patient, *The Love Cure: Therapy Erotic and Sexual* is a must read! John challenges the puritanically restrictive notions of therapy, while meeting the ethical dilemmas that these challenges raise.

If after considering these titles you're still feeling a loss of energy and desire, SPRING suggests you consider *In Midlife: A Jungian Perspective by Murray Stein*.

We also have some audio tapes to turn up the heat and warm your soul. The *Erotic Poems of the Earl of Rochester*, read by the Obie-award winning Ian Magilton, is marvelous. You'll discover why smart schoolboys always managed to find the Earl's long suppressed poems. Charles II's drinking pal and poet was bawdy and raucous, but as elegant as only rakes of the Restoration could be.

Want even more elegance? *Gaius Valerius Catullus's Complete Poetic Works*, translated by Jacob Rabinowitz, is a bold translation that captures the passion of pagan Rome. William S. Burroughs says of this work, "Beautifully translated...trivial, frivolous, profound obscene. Hear the fossils of lust."

And in *Pink Madness*, James Hillman takes on the most loaded topic of the nineties—pornography, in a way you would not believe. You have to hear it!

To order any of the above call *(860) 974-3428*,
fax *(860) 974-3195*
E-mail *Spring@neca.com*
Visa and Mastercard accepted or just send check postal order to:

Spring Publications, Inc.
299 East Quassett Rd.
Woodstock, Connecticut 06281

and check out our website at
http://www.neca.com/~spring

UNLOCK THE ESSENTIAL MYSTERY
AT THE CENTER OF YOUR LIFE

THE
SOUL'S
CODE
IN SEARCH OF
CHARACTER
AND CALLING

JAMES HILLMAN

What were you meant to do?
What is your life's calling?

Using the biographies of some
of the world's most extraordinary
people, Hillman shows how
seemingly insignificant events
of your past can be signposts
toward your destiny.

A Selection of the Book-of-the-Month Club
Also available as a Random House AudioBook

RANDOM HOUSE
http://www.randomhouse.com/

BUDDHISM
and the
Art of
Psychotherapy

Hayao Kawai
Foreword by David H. Rosen

Japan's first Jungian psychoanalyst examines his own experience of reconciling the
Buddhist culture he had abandoned with
the Jungianism he adopted during his
education in the West. Describing how
he has utilized some elements of Buddhism to initiate a mutual process of individual development, Kawai provides an
inspiring view of therapeutic transformation, in which Eastern and Western perspectives provide a richer view of our existence. $22.95

Texas A&M University Press
Drawer C • College Station, Texas 77843-4354
800-826-8911 • FAX: 409-847-8752 • http://www.tamu.edu/upress/

Roundtable Sessions for 1997

The Eranos Conferences

in beautiful Ascona, Switzerland

L'anima e l'abitazione
(in Italian)

May 8-11, 1997

Chroniclers and Shamans:
Events and Archetypal Images
(in English)

June 4-8, 1997

Chroniclers and Shamans refers to the *I Ching*, hexagram 57, second line. This line stands for two fundamentally different ways of perceiving a psychological situation; one through the recorded outer facts and the other through confronting the archetypal images in dreams or responses to an oracle (i.e. the *I Ching*). These two modes are useful in individual therapeutic analysis as well as in dealing with the collective past.

Traditional Ties and Global Nets:
The Interplay of Individual and Collective
Identity
(in English)

October 22-26, 1997

Sponsored by the Eranos Foundation and
the Uehiro Foundation on Ethics and Education

a memoir of dying . . .

a Jungian therapist's moving memoir of coming to terms with her diagnosis of stage IV metastatic breast cancer—in essence, a death sentence.

"Christina Middlebrook offers her hand to others with the illness, accompanying them down its path. She also makes unmistakably clear what the help and love of family, friends, support group members, physicians, and nurses means to someone who is ill." —DAVID SPIEGEL, M.D.

"Along with her harrowing chronicle of the progress of her recurring cancer and the desperate battle to beat it back. . . Middlebrook reveals a slow and equally painful process of inner growth. And not the kind of psychobabble she disdains as 'New Age tyranny'. . .but rather a deeper, more philosophic recognition of harsh but essential reality. . .Her brave book is a gift."
—SAN FRANCISCO CHRONICLE

"Speaking of her own inevitable death with incredible candor and humor, Christina Middlebrook reminds us of what life is all about. For the reader, this is a formidable gift when he or she least expects it."
—SLAVENKA DRAKULIC, author of *The Balkan Express*

$22.00 at bookstores or call:
1 800-331-3761

SEEING THE CRAB

Christina Middlebrook

BasicBooks
A Division of HarperCollins*Publishers*

Get 'em while they're cold ...

Spring 53 (**Pagans, Christians, Jews**): Jung's secret initiation into Mithraism. James Hillman on "How Jewish is Archetypal Psychology?" Oracles. Disability. Vampires.

Spring 54 (**The Reality Issue**): Wolfgang Giegerich on killing for consciousness. Edward S. Casey on Reality. Automatic Writing. Hillman's updating of "Alchemical Blue."

Spring 55 (**The Issue from Hell**): Sheila Grimaldi-Craig's "Whipping the Chthonic Woman." "The Children of Hell." Max Nordau's *Degeneration.* "Reading Jung Backwards."

Spring 56 (**Who Was Zwingli?**): Hillman's "Once More into the Fray" takes on Wolfgang Giegrich. Benjamin Sells on Lawyer's Ethics. David Miller on Joseph Campbell. Jung's *Zarathusthra* Seminar, and the first Index to *Spring* in years!

Spring 57 (**Archetypal Sex**): Rachel Pollack on Transsexuals. Hillman on Pornography. John Haule on Erotic Analysis. Sonu Shamdasani on who really wrote Jung's memoirs.

Spring 58 (**Disillusionment**): Joseph Landry on Alcoholics Anonymous, Connie Zweig on Transcendental Meditators, David L. Hart on meeting Jung for the first time, James Hillman on the need to falsify or disguise the story of your life.

Spring 59 (**Opening the Dreamway**): Robert Duncan on what Jung and Hillman meant to his poetry, Nor Hall on Robert Duncan and Jess, Charles Boer on how Gods guide the minds of poets ancient and modern, James Hillman on heroes, Michael Adams on why Jungians hate semiotics.

Each issue is still available (for $17.50) but to subscribers (or renewers)
they're only $12 each.
Get all 7 (while they last) for just $60 — a savings of $24!
We pay postage and shipping worldwide :

Spring Journal
Box 583
Putnam, CT 06260

Since 1941, **Spring**
is the oldest Jungian journal in the world.
For over fifty years it has been bringing
professionals and the general reader
new ideas
in depth and archetypal psychology,
sometimes radical, sometimes
conservative, but always fresh,
interesting, elegant —
and sometimes even fun!

Subscribe to **Spring**
and *save* over 1/3 off
the cover cost.

We publish twice a year.
A single issue costs $17.50 but
a subscription (two issues) is only $24,
and we'll pay postage and shipping worldwide.

Send check, credit card number or postal order for $24
(Mastercard and Visa accepted) to:

Spring Journal
Box 583
Putnam, CT 06260